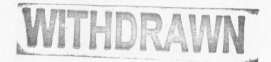

THE WORKS OF

John Ruskin

(IN 22 VOLUMES)

THE

ELEMENTS OF DRAWING.

THE

ELEMENTS OF DRAWING

IN

THREE LETTERS TO BEGINNERS

BY

JOHN RUSKIN, LL.D.

HONORARY STUDENT OF CHRIST CHURCH, AND HONORARY FELLOW OF
CORPUS CHRISTI COLLEGE, OXFORD, ETC. ETC.

WITH ILLUSTRATIONS
Drawn by the Author

WITH AN INTRODUCTION BY CHARLES ELIOT NORTON

BRANTWOOD EDITION

MAYNARD, MERRILL, & CO., NEW YORK
GEORGE ALLEN, LONDON AND ORPINGTON

Reprinted 1972
Scholarly Press, Inc., 22929 Industrial Drive East
St. Clair Shores, Michigan 48080

Library of Congress Cataloging in Publication Data

Ruskin, John, 1819-1900.
    The elements of drawing in three letters to beginners

    Reprint of the 1893 ed.
    1. Drawing. I. Title.
NC710.R8 1972   741'.01   74-115264
ISBN 0-403-00307-5

SPECIAL ANNOUNCEMENT.

[" The Elements of Drawing " was written during the winter of 1856. The First Edition was published in 1857 ; the Second followed in the same year, with some additions and slight alterations. The Third Edition consisted of sixth thousand, 1859 ; seventh thousand, 1860 ; and eighth thousand, 1861.

The work was partly reproduced in "Our Sketching Club," by the Rev. R. St. John Tyrwhitt, M.A., 1874 ; with new editions in 1875, 1882, and 1886.

Mr. Ruskin meant, during his tenure of the Slade Professorship at Oxford, to recast his teaching, and to write a systematic manual for the use of his Drawing School, under the title of "The Laws of Fésole." Of this only vol. i. was completed, 1879 ; second edition, 1882.

As, therefore, "The Elements of Drawing" has never been completely superseded, and as many readers of Mr. Ruskin's works have expressed a desire to possess the book in its old form, it is now reprinted as it stood in 1859, with the addition of an Index.]

INTRODUCTION.

THE chief aim of this little book is to teach the student *to see* truly—"the sight is a more important thing than the drawing." "To read and write comes by nature," it is true, but not so, to see; the eye needs training to use aright the faculty of vision. Few acquisitions are more desirable, for truth of sight indefinitely increases the enjoyment of life, while it also helps to form and regulate mental judgments, and to refine and cultivate the taste. To learn to draw is to teach the eye to see, and the hand to represent truly the images of sight, but the popular modes of instruction in drawing tend often not to make the sight more true, but rather to destroy its capacity to see correctly, and to prevent the pupil from ever properly appreciating either the aspects of nature or the finer qualities of art.

Mr. Ruskin, possessing by birth very remarkable powers of sight, and having been wisely trained in their exercise from his earliest years, acquired a mastery of draughtsmanship such, in some particulars, as few of the greatest artists have attained. For several years he gave instruction in drawing in the Workingmen's College in London, and this book contains the result of his experience of methods and of practice. It is the work of a master by right not alone of extraordinary gifts, but as well by right of long experience, and of knowledge gained by that patience of toil which is the final proof and test of genius. In this, as in other works of his, he may be at times, through idiosyncrasy of temperament, or other cause, a questionable guide; but in the spirit and general direction of his teaching, no less than in specific detail, he is always an inspiring and often an incomparable instructor.

The book was first published in 1857. Twenty years afterward Mr. Ruskin published the first part of another treatise on the elementary principles and practice of drawing and painting—"The Laws of Fésolé"—which was intended, when complete, to contain all that was permanently valuable

in the " Elements of Drawing," together
with such further guidance as his observation had shown to be necessary. The two
books should be studied together, and if well
studied cannot but be of service to the resolute student, such as in many respects no
other manual of drawing can render.

But no teaching of drawing can make an
artist—that is, can enable the pupil to acquire the power of pictorial expression of
thought, any more than the study of the
forms and methods of poetry can enable
him to become a poet. Few among the pro-
fessional painters of to-day draw correctly;
they neither see truly nor delineate what
they see; and yet their works are praised,
are admired, are bought. And the pictures
of the few who can draw correctly are, for
the most part, not expressions of intellect
or imagination, but mere representations of
semblances reflected from the mindless mirror of the eye.

Yet though no teaching can make an artist
in the full sense of the word, drawing should
form a part of every system of thorough
education; for besides the general quicken-

ing of perception and the training of the
eye to accuracy of sight which it gives,
it affords the means of recording transient
scenes and of noting the forms of objects,
such as no written description can secure,
and no words can convey to others. At its
lowest estimate it is an accomplishment perhaps larger in resources of pleasure than any
other, and at its highest it affords a mode of
expression second only to that of language
itself, and superior to language in the respects which have just been indicated. Photography can in part supply its place, but can
by no means serve as a complete substitute
for it, either as discipline of the sight or as
a record of personal impressions.

The vast extension of illustration in books
and magazines during the last few years, and
the prospect of still further increase in the
use of engraving of every sort, enhance the
need of instruction in drawing as an element
in popular education, if only as the means
by which correct appreciation of this mode
of appeal to the intelligence may be acquired. The mind may be mistaught by
illustrations addressed to the eye, no less

than by words addressed to the ear, or read
on the printed page. Many of the illustrations daily offered in journals and magazines
are harmful through falsehood, and for the
detection of this falsehood some knowledge
of the principles of drawing is needed.

By the study of these books of Mr. Ruskin's this knowledge may be acquired to a
considerable and useful degree even by those
who have not opportunity or ability to learn
and practise the art of drawing itself. Quite
apart from the specific instruction to the
student of drawing as to methods and material, a great part of the "Elements" and
of the "Laws of Fésolé" is given to the
exposition of the principles of pictorial art
—of line, of light and shade, of colour, of
composition—illustrated by examples of the
work of masters. And this portion of the
books, while of primary value to the reader
who may desire to learn how to discriminate
good work from bad, and to judge of the
merit of engraving or of picture, is of hardly
less worth to the student of literary art.
For the principles of expression in the various arts are not different in essence, but differ

only as the arts are conditioned by the different material which they employ, by the means they have at control, and by the methods of work appropriate to their specific nature. The laws of beauty do not vary in one form of creative art from another; it is only in the method of appeal to the intelligence that the arts differ. The laws of beautiful colour, of beautiful form, of beautiful sound, are not merely analogous, but may be resolved into the same ultimate principles. Words are imperfect to express the differences in the application of these principles in the different arts; we must use the same words for all. Proportion, harmony, rhythm belong equally to the arts of the ear and the eye; and even when the arts require special terms for the definition of their specific qualities, a close analogy underlies the respective nomenclatures. The arts mutually illustrate each other, and the understanding of the laws of poetic composition in literature helps to the understanding of poetic composition in painting or in sculpture. The same conditions effect similar results in all the arts. The work of Phidias is of the same order with the work

of Sophocles; that of Praxiteles and Scopas
is closely akin to that of Euripides. The
same age produced the cycle of French ro-
mance and the cathedrals of the Ile de
France. Hogarth and Fielding express
themselves and their age in different arts
but in similar manner. Turner and Scott are
contemporaries in expression; the sources
of their poetic inspiration are largely the
same, and their very methods in their respective arts are often curiously analogous.

I know of no better book than these "Elements" to put into the hands of one who de-
sires to form a correct judgment concerning
the engravings and pictures which every day
puts before his eyes. The latter half of it is
full of criticism of works of Dürer, Leonardo
da Vinci, Turner, and many others, which is
helpful in wider application. To learn the
qualities of an engraving by Dürer, or an
etching by Rembrandt or Turner, is a lesson
of no limited worth. If rightly learned, it is
to gain the power of appreciation of all work
of the representative arts. But more than
this, by the study of the expression of the
poetic faculty in the productions of a great

artist, the enjoyment of nature no less than of art is disciplined and increased, the dormant faculties of the imagination are roused into activity, and the circle of intellectual resources is indefinitely widened.

Mr. Ruskin's own work as a draughtsman cannot be too much studied. Some, however, of the specimens of it which have been published in recent years fail to do justice to it. But the engravings from his drawings which he himself in his best years gave to the public cannot be too highly prized as pieces of draughtsmanship and of engraving. The original editions of " Modern Painters," of the " Stones of Venice," of the " Seven Lamps of Architecture," and of " Examples of the Architecture of Venice," contain engravings which in their kind have never been surpassed, and are not likely to be rivalled. The drawing shows an exquisiteness of touch combined with perfect firmness of hand, guided by the finest perception, and the reproduction of these qualities in the engraving leaves nothing to be desired. Whoever possesses these plates, or even one of them, as originally published, possesses a work of art of the highest order in its kind.

In the recently published Life of Mr. Ruskin, by Mr. W. G. Collingwood, the reader will find much valuable and interesting information respecting Mr. Ruskin's methods and practice of drawing, and will learn how varied and accomplished his work as a draughtsman has been, and how great an influence he has exerted upon contemporary art.

C. E. N.

SHADY HILL, CAMBRIDGE, MASS.,
    May, 1893.

ADVERTISEMENT

TO

THE SECOND EDITION.

———◆———

As one or two questions, asked of me since the publication of this work, have indicated points requiring elucidation, I have added a few short notes in the first Appendix. It is not, I think, desirable otherwise to modify the form or add to the matter of a book as it passes through successive editions; I have, therefore, only mended the wording of some obscure sentences; with which exception the text remains, and will remain, in its original form, which I had carefully considered. Should the public find the book useful, and call for further editions of it, such additional notes

as may be necessary will be always placed
in the first Appendix, where they can be at
once referred to, in any library, by the pos-
sessors of the earlier editions ; and I will take
care they shall not be numerous.

August 3, 1857.

PREFACE.

———◆———

i. IT may perhaps be thought, that in prefacing a manual of drawing, I ought to expatiate on the reasons why drawing should be learned; but those reasons appear to me so many and so weighty, that I cannot quickly state or enforce them. With the reader's permission, as this volume is too large already, I will waive all discussion respecting the importance of the subject, and touch only on those points which may appear questionable in the method of its treatment.

ii. In the first place, the book is not calculated for the use of children under the age of twelve or fourteen. I do not think it advisable to engage a child in any but the most voluntary practice of art. If it has talent for drawing, it will be continually scrawling on what paper it can get; and should be allowed to scrawl at its own free will, due praise being given for every appearance of care, or truth, in its efforts. It should be allowed to amuse itself with cheap colours almost as soon as it has sense enough to wish for them. If it merely daubs the paper with shapeless stains, the colour-box may be taken away till it knows better: but as soon as it begins painting red coats on soldiers, striped flags to ships, &c., it should have colours at command; and, without restraining its choice of subject in that imaginative and historical art, of a military tendency, which children delight in, (generally quite as valuable, by the way, as any historical art delighted in by their elders,) it should be gently led by the parents to try to draw, in such childish fashion as may be, the things it can see and likes,— birds, or butterflies, or flowers, or fruit.

iii. In later years, the indulgence of using the colour should only be granted as a reward, after it has shown care and progress in its drawings with pencil. A limited number of good and amusing prints should always be within a boy's reach: in these days of cheap illustration he can hardly possess a volume

of nursery tales without good woodcuts in it,
and should be encouraged to copy what he
likes best of this kind; but should be firmly
restricted to a *few* prints and to a few books.
If a child has many toys, it will get tired of
them and break them; if a boy has many
prints he will merely dawdle and scrawl over
them; it is by the limitation of the number
of his possessions that his pleasure in them
is perfected, and his attention concentrated.
The parents need give themselves no trouble
in instructing him, as far as drawing is concerned, beyond insisting upon economical and
neat habits with his colours and paper, showing him the best way of holding pencil and
rule, and, so far as they take notice of his
work, pointing out where a line is too short
or too long, or too crooked, when compared
with the copy; *accuracy* being the first and
last thing they look for. If the child shows
talent for inventing or grouping figures, the
parents should neither check, nor praise it.
They may laugh with it frankly, or show
pleasure in what it has done, just as they
show pleasure in seeing it well, or cheerful;
but they must not praise it for being clever,

b

any more than they would praise it for being stout. They should praise it only for what costs it self-denial, namely attention and hard work; otherwise they will make it work for vanity's sake, and always badly. The best books to put into its hands are those illustrated by George Cruikshank or by Richter. (See Appendix.) At about the age of twelve or fourteen, it is quite time enough to set youth or girl to serious work; and then this book will, I think, be useful to them; and I have good hope it may be so, likewise, to persons of more advanced age wishing to know something of the first principles of art.

iv. Yet observe, that the method of study recommended is not brought forward as absolutely the best, but only as the best which I can at present devise for an isolated student. It is very likely that farther experience in teaching may enable me to modify it with advantage in several important respects; but I am sure the main principles of it are sound, and most of the exercises as useful as they can be rendered without a master's superintendence. The method differs, however, so

materially from that generally adopted by drawing-masters, that a word or two of explanation
may be needed to justify what might otherwise be thought wilful eccentricity.

v. The manuals at present published on the
subject of drawing are all directed, as far as I
know, to one or other of two objects. Either
they propose to give the student a power of
dexterous sketching with pencil or water-
colour, so as to emulate (at considerable distance) the slighter work of our second-rate
artists; or they propose to give him such
accurate command of mathematical forms as
may afterwards enable him to design rapidly
and cheaply for manufactures. When drawing is taught as an accomplishment, the first
is the aim usually proposed; while the second
is the object kept chiefly in view at Marlborough House, and in the branch Government
Schools of Design.

vi. Of the fitness of the modes of study
adopted in those schools, to the end specially
intended, judgment is hardly yet possible;
only, it seems to me, that we are all too much
in the habit of confusing art as *applied* to
manufacture, with manufacture itself. For

instance, the skill by which an inventive workman designs and moulds a beautiful cup, is skill of true art; but the skill by which that cup is copied and afterwards multiplied a thousandfold, is skill of manufacture: and the faculties which enable one workman to design and elaborate his original piece, are not to be developed by the same system of instruction as those which enable another to produce a maximum number of approximate copies of it in a given time. Farther: it is surely inexpedient that any reference to purposes of manufacture should interfere with the education of the artist himself. Try first to manufacture a Raphael; then let Raphael direct your manufacture. He will design you a plate, or cup, or a house, or a palace, whenever you want it, and design them in the most convenient and rational way; but do not let your anxiety to reach the platter and the cup interfere with your education of the Raphael. Obtain first the best work you can, and the ablest hands, irrespective of any consideration of economy or facility of production. Then leave your trained artist to determine how far art can be popularised, or manufacture ennobled.

vii. Now, I believe that (irrespective of differences in individual temper and character) the
excellence of an artist, as such, depends
wholly on refinement of perception, and that
it is this, mainly, which a master or a school
can teach; so that while powers of invention
distinguish man from man, powers of perception distinguish school from school. All
great schools enforce delicacy of drawing and
subtlety of sight: and the only rule which I
have, as yet, found to be without exception respecting art, is that all great art is
delicate.

viii. Therefore, the chief aim and bent of the
following system is to obtain, first, a perfectly
patient, and, to the utmost of the pupil's
power, a delicate method of work, such as
may ensure his seeing truly. For I am nearly
convinced, that when once we see keenly
enough, there is very little difficulty in drawing what we see; but, even supposing that
this difficulty be still great, I believe that the
sight is a more important thing than the drawing; and I would rather teach drawing that
my pupils may learn to love Nature, than
teach the looking at Nature that they may

learn to draw. It is surely also a more
important thing, for young people and unpro-
fessional students, to know how to appreciate
the art of others, than to gain much power in
art themselves. Now the modes of sketching
ordinarily taught are inconsistent with this
power of judgment. No person trained to the
superficial execution of modern water-colour
painting, can understand the work of Titian
or Leonardo; they must for ever remain blind
to the refinement of such men's pencilling, and
the precision of their thinking. But, however slight a degree of manipulative power
the student may reach by pursuing the mode
recommended to him in these letters, I will
answer for it that he cannot go once through
the advised exercises without beginning to
understand what masterly work means; and,
by the time he has gained some proficiency in
them, he will have a pleasure in looking at
the painting of the great schools, and a new
perception of the exquisiteness of natural
scenery, such as would repay him for much
more labour than I have asked him to
undergo.

ix. That labour is, nevertheless, sufficiently

irksome, nor is it possible that it should be otherwise, so long as the pupil works unassisted by a master. For the smooth and straight road which admits unembarrassed progress must, I fear, be dull as well as smooth ; and the hedges need to be close and trim when there is no guide to warn or bring back the erring traveller. The system followed in this work will, therefore, at first, surprise somewhat sorrowfully those who are familiar with the practice of our class at the Working Men's College; for there, the pupil, having the master at his side to extricate him from such embarrassments as his first efforts may lead into, is *at once* set to draw from a solid object, and soon finds entertainment in his efforts and interest in his difficulties. Of course the simplest object which it is possible to set before the eye is a sphere ; and, practically, I find a child's toy, a white leather ball, better than anything else; as the gradations on balls of plaster of Paris, which I use sometimes to try the strength of pupils who have had previous practice, are a little too delicate for a beginner to perceive. It has been objected that a circle, or the outline of a sphere, is one of the most difficult of all lines to draw. It is so; * but I do not want it to be drawn. All that his study of the ball is to teach the pupil, is the way in which shade gives the appearance of projection. This he learns most satisfactorily from a sphere; because any solid form, terminated by straight lines or flat surfaces, owes some of its appearance of projection to its perspective; but in the sphere, what, without shade, was a flat circle, becomes, merely by the added shade, the image of a solid ball; and this fact is just as striking to the learner, whether his circular outline be true or false. He is, therefore, never allowed to trouble himself about it; if he makes the ball look as oval as an egg, the degree of error is simply pointed out to him, and he does better next time, and better still the next. But his mind is always fixed on the gradation of shade, and the outline left to take, in due time, care of itself. I call it outline, for the sake of immediate intelligibility, —strictly speaking, it is merely the edge of the shade; no pupil in my class being ever

---

* Or, more accurately, appears to be so, because any one can see an error in a circle.

allowed to draw an outline, in the ordinary sense. It is pointed out to him, from the first, that Nature relieves one mass, or one tint, against another; but outlines none. The outline exercise, the second suggested in this letter, is recommended, not to enable the pupil to draw outlines, but as the only means by which, unassisted, he can test his accuracy of eye, and discipline his hand. When the master is by, errors in the form and extent of shadows can be pointed out as easily as in outline, and the handling can be gradually corrected in details of the work. But the solitary student can only find out his own mistakes by help of the traced limit, and can only test the firmness of his hand by an exercise in which nothing but firmness is required; and during which all other considerations (as of softness, complexity, &c.) are entirely excluded.

x. Both the system adopted at the Working Men's College, and that recommended here, agree, however, in one principle, which I consider the most important and special of all that are involved in my teaching: namely, the attaching its full importance, from the

first, to local colour.   I believe that the endeavour to separate, in the course of instruction,
the observation of light and shade from that
of local colour, has always been, and must
always be, destructive of the student's power
of accurate sight, and that it corrupts his taste
as much as it retards his progress.   I will not
occupy the reader's time by any discussion of
the principle here, but I wish him to note it as
the only distinctive one in my system, so far
as it *is* a system.   For the recommendation
to the pupil to copy faithfully, and without
alteration, whatever natural object he chooses
to study, is serviceable, among other reasons,
just because it gets rid of systematic rules
altogether, and teaches people to draw, as
country lads learn to ride, without saddle
or stirrups; my main object being, at first,
not to get my pupils to hold their reins
prettily, but to "sit like a jackanapes, never
off."

xi. In these written instructions, therefore,
it has always been with regret that I have
seen myself forced to advise anything like
monotonous or formal discipline.   But, to
the unassisted student, such formalities are

indispensable, and I am not without hope that the sense of secure advancement, and the pleasure of independent effort, may render the following out of even the more tedious exercises here proposed, possible to the solitary learner, without weariness. But if it should be otherwise, and he finds the first steps painfully irksome, I can only desire him to consider whether the acquirement of so great a power as that of pictorial expression of thought be not worth some toil; or whether it is likely, in the natural order of matters in this working world, that so great a gift should be attainable by those who will give no price for it.

xii. One task, however, of some difficulty, the student will find I have not imposed upon him : namely, learning the laws of perspective. It would be worth while to learn them, if he could do so easily; but without a master's help, and in the way perspective is at present explained in treatises, the difficulty is greater than the gain. For perspective is not of the slightest use, except in rudimentary work. You can draw the rounding line of a table in perspective, but you cannot draw the sweep

of a sea bay; you can foreshorten a log of
wood by it, but you cannot foreshorten an
arm.   Its laws are too gross and few to be
applied to any subtle form; therefore, as you
must learn to draw the subtle forms by the
eye, certainly you may draw the simple ones.
No great painters ever trouble themselves
about perspective, and very few of them know
its laws; they draw everything by the eye,
and, naturally enough, disdain in the easy
parts of their work rules which cannot help
them in difficult ones.   It would take about a
month's labour to draw imperfectly, by laws
of perspective, what any great Venetian will
draw perfectly in five minutes, when he is
throwing a wreath of leaves round a head, or
bending the curves of a pattern in and out
among the folds of drapery.   It is true that
when perspective was first discovered, everybody amused themselves with it; and all the
great painters put fine saloons and arcades
behind their Madonnas, merely to show that
they could draw in perspective: but even this
was generally done by them only to catch the
public eye, and they disdained the perspective
so much, that though they took the greatest

pains with the circlet of a crown, or the rim
of a crystal cup, in the heart of their picture,
they would twist their capitals of columns
and towers of churches about in the background in the most wanton way, wherever
they liked the lines to go, provided only they
left just perspective enough to please the
public.

xiii. In modern days, I doubt if any artist
among us, except David Roberts, knows so
much perspective as would enable him to
draw a Gothic arch to scale at a given angle
and distance.   Turner, though he was pro-
fessor of perspective to the Royal Academy,
did not know what he professed, and never,
as far as I remember, drew a single building
in true perspective in his life; he drew them
only with as much perspective as suited him.
Prout also knew nothing of perspective, and
twisted his buildings, as Turner did, into
whatever shapes he liked.   I do not justify
this; and would recommend the student at
least to treat perspective with common civility,
but to pay no court to it.   The best way he
can learn it, by himself, is by taking a pane of
glass, fixed in a frame, so that it can be set

upright before the eye, at the distance at which the proposed sketch is intended to be seen. Let the eye be placed at some fixed point, opposite the middle of the pane of glass, but as high or as low as the student likes; then with a brush at the end of a stick, and a little body-colour that will adhere to the glass, the lines of the landscape may be traced on the glass, as you see them through it. When so traced they are all in true perspective. If the glass be sloped in any direction, the lines are still in true perspective, only it is perspective calculated for a sloping plane, while common perspective always supposes the plane of the picture to be vertical. It is good, in early practice, to accustom yourself to enclose your subject, before sketching it, with a light frame of wood held upright before you; it will show you what you may legitimately take into your picture, and what choice there is between a narrow foreground near you, and a wide one farther off; also, what height of tree or building you can properly take in, &c.*

* If the student is fond of architecture, and wishes to know more of perspective than he can learn in this rough way, Mr. Runciman (of 49 Acacia Road, St. John's

xiv. Of figure drawing, nothing is said in the following pages, because I do not think figures, as chief subjects, can be drawn to any good purpose by an amateur. As accessaries in landscape, they are just to be drawn on the same principles as anything else.

xv. Lastly: If any of the directions given subsequently to the student should be found obscure by him, or if at any stage of the recommended practice he find himself in difficulties which I have not enough provided against, he may apply by letter to Mr. Ward, who is my under drawing-master at the Working Men's College (45 Great Ormond Street), and who will give any required assistance, on the lowest terms that can remunerate him for the occupation of his time. I have not leisure myself in general to answer letters of inquiry, however much I may desire to do so; but Mr. Ward has always the power of referring any question to me when he thinks it necessary. I have good hope, however,

Wood), who was my first drawing-master, and to whom I owe many happy hours, can teach it him quickly, easily, and rightly. [Mr. Runciman has died since this was written: Mr. Ward's present address is Bedford Chambers, 28 Southampton Street, Strand, London, W.C.]

that enough guidance is given in this work to prevent the occurrence of any serious embarrassment ; and I believe that the student who obeys its directions will find, on the whole, that the best answerer of questions is perseverance ; and the best drawing-masters are the woods and hills.

[1857.]

CONTENTS.

—◆—

THE
ELEMENTS OF DRAWING.

LETTER I.

ON FIRST PRACTICE.

1. MY DEAR READER,—Whether this book is
to be of use to you or not, depends wholly on
your reason for wishing to learn to draw.   If
you desire only to possess a graceful accomplishment, to be able to converse in a fluent manner
about drawing, or to amuse yourself listlessly
in listless hours, I cannot help you: but if you
wish to learn drawing that you may be able to
set down clearly, and usefully, records of such
things as cannot be described in words, either
to assist your own memory of them, or to convey
distinct ideas of them to other people; if you
wish to obtain quicker perceptions of the beauty

A *

of the natural world, and to preserve something like a true image of beautiful things that pass away, or which you must yourself leave; if, also, you wish to understand the minds of great painters, and to be able to appreciate their work sincerely, seeing it for yourself, and loving it, not merely taking up the thoughts of other people about it; then I *can* help you, or, which is better, show you how to help yourself.

2. Only you must understand, first of all, that these powers, which indeed are noble and desirable, cannot be got without work. It is much easier to learn to draw well, than it is to learn to play well on any musical instrument; but you know that it takes three or four years of practice, giving three or four hours a day, to acquire even ordinary command over the keys of a piano; and you must not think that a masterly command of your pencil, and the knowledge of what may be done with it, can be acquired without painstaking, or in a *very* short time. The kind of drawing which is taught, or supposed to be taught, in our schools, in a term or two, perhaps at the rate of an hour's practice a week, is not drawing at all. It is only the performance of a few dexterous (not always even that) evolutions

on paper with a black-lead pencil; profitless alike to performer and beholder, unless as a matter of vanity, and that the smallest possible vanity. If any young person, after being taught what is, in polite circles, called "drawing," will try to copy the commonest piece of real work —suppose a lithograph on the titlepage of a new opera air, or a woodcut in the cheapest illustrated newspaper of the day,—they will find themselves entirely beaten. And yet that common lithograph was drawn with coarse chalk, much more difficult to manage than the pencil of which an accomplished young lady is supposed to have command; and that woodcut was drawn in urgent haste, and half spoiled in the cutting afterwards; and both were done by people whom nobody thinks of as artists, or praises for their power; both were done for daily bread, with no more artist's pride than any simple handicraftsmen feel in the work they live by.

3. Do not, therefore, think that you can learn drawing, any more than a new language, without some hard and disagreeable labour. But do not, on the other hand, if you are ready and willing to pay this price, fear that you may be

unable to get on for want of special talent. It
is indeed true that the persons who have peculiar talent for art, draw instinctively, and get on
almost without teaching ; though never without
toil. It is true, also, that of inferior talent for
drawing there are many degrees : it will take
one person a much longer time than another to
attain the same results, and the results thus
painfully attained are never quite so satisfactory
as those got with greater ease when the faculties
are naturally adapted to the study. But I have
never yet, in the experiments I have made, met
with a person who could not learn to draw at
all ; and, in general, there is a satisfactory and
available power in every one to learn drawing
if he wishes, just as nearly all persons have the
power of learning French, Latin, or arithmetic,
in a decent and useful degree, if their lot in life
requires them to possess such knowledge.

4. Supposing then that you are ready to take
a certain amount of pains, and to bear a little
irksomeness and a few disappointments bravely,
I can promise you that an hour's practice a day
for six months, or an hour's practice every other
day for twelve months, or, disposed in whatever
way you find convenient, some hundred and fifty

hours' practice, will give you sufficient power of
drawing faithfully whatever you want to draw,
and a good judgment, up to a certain point, of
other people's work : of which hours if you have
one to spare at present, we may as well begin
at once.

EXERCISE I.

5. Everything that you can see in the world
around you, presents itself to your eyes only as
an arrangement of patches of different colours
variously shaded.[1] Some of these patches of

[1] (*N. B.*—This note is only for the satisfaction of incredu-
lous or curious readers. You may miss it if you are in a hurry,
or are willing to take the statement in the text on trust.)

The perception of solid Form is entirely a matter of experience. We *see* nothing but flat colours ; and it is only by a
series of experiments that we find out that a stain of black
or grey indicates the dark side of a solid substance, or that a
faint hue indicates that the object in which it appears is far
away. The whole technical power of painting depends on our
recovery of what may be called the *innocence of the eye ;* that
is to say, of a sort of childish perception of these flat stains of
colour, merely as such, without consciousness of what they
signify,—as a blind man would see them if suddenly gifted
with sight.

For instance : when grass is lighted strongly by the sun in
certain directions, it is turned from green into a peculiar and
somewhat dusty-looking yellow. If we had been born blind,
and were suddenly endowed with sight on a piece of grass thus
lighted in some parts by the sun, it would appear to us that

colour have an appearance of lines or texture
within them, as a piece of cloth or silk has of
threads, or an animal's skin shows texture of
hairs : but whether this be the case or not, the
first broad aspect of the thing is that of a patch
of some definite colour ; and the first thing to be
learned is, how to produce extents of smooth
colour, without texture.

6. This can only be done properly with a
brush ; but a brush, being soft at the point,
causes so much uncertainty in the touch of an
unpractised hand, that it is hardly possible to
learn to draw first with it, and it is better to

part of the grass was green, and part a dusty yellow (very
nearly of the colour of primroses) ; and, if there were primroses near, we should think that the sunlighted grass was
another mass of plants of the same sulphur-yellow colour.
We should try to gather some of them, and then find that the
colour went away from the grass when we stood between it
and the sun, but not from the primroses ; and by a series of
experiments we should find out that the sun was really the
cause of the colour in the one,—not in the other. We go
through such processes of experiment unconsciously in childhood ; and having once come to conclusions touching the
signification of certain colours, we always suppose that we
see what we only know, and have hardly any consciousness
of the real aspect of the signs we have learned to interpret.
Very few people have any idea that sunlighted grass is yellow.

Now, a highly accomplished artist has always reduced himself as nearly as possible to this condition of infantine sight.

take, in early practice, some instrument with a hard and fine point, both that we may give some support to the hand, and that by working over the subject with so delicate a point, the attention may be properly directed to all the most minute parts of it.   Even the best artists need occasionally to study subjects with a pointed instrument, in order thus to discipline their attention : and a beginner must be content to do so for a considerable period.

7. Also, observe that before we trouble ourselves about differences of colour, we must be able to lay on *one* colour properly, in whatever

---

He sees the colours of nature exactly as they are, and therefore perceives at once in the sunlighted grass the precise relation between the two colours that form its shade and light. To him it does not seem shade and light, but bluish green barred with gold.

Strive, therefore, first of all, to convince yourself of this great fact about sight.   This, in your hand, which you know by experience and touch to be a book, is to your eye nothing but a patch of white, variously gradated and spotted ; this other thing near you, which by experience you know to be a table, is to your eye only a patch of brown, variously darkened and veined ; and so on : and the whole art of Painting consists merely in perceiving the shape and depth of these patches of colour, and putting patches of the same size, depth, and shape on canvas.   The only obstacle to the success of painting is, that many of the real colours are brighter and paler than it is possible to put on canvas : we must put darker ones to represent them.

gradations of depth and whatever shapes **we**
want. We will try, therefore, first to lay on
tints or patches of grey, of whatever depth we
want, with a pointed instrument. Take any
finely pointed steel pen (one of Gillott's lithographic crowquills is best), and a piece of quite
smooth, but not shining, note-paper, cream laid,
and get some ink that has stood already some
time in the inkstand, so as to be quite black,

a   *b*

FIG. 1.

and as thick as it can be without clogging the
pen. Take a rule, and draw four straight lines,
so as to enclose a square, or nearly a square,
about as large as *a*, Fig. 1. I say nearly a
square, because it does not in the least matter
whether it is quite square or not, the object
being merely to get a space enclosed by straight
lines.

8. Now, try to fill in that square space with
crossed lines, so completely and evenly that it
shall look like a square patch of grey silk or

cloth, cut out and laid on the white paper, as
at *b*.   Cover it quickly, first with straightish
lines, in any direction you like, not troubling
yourself to draw them much closer or neater
than those in the square *a*.   Let them quite dry
before retouching them.   (If you draw three or
four squares side by side, you may always be
going on with one while the others are drying.)
Then cover these lines with others in a different
direction, and let those dry; then in another
direction still, and let those dry.   Always wait
long enough to run no risk of blotting, and then
draw the lines as quickly as you can.   Each
ought to be laid on as swiftly as the dash of the
pen of a good writer; but if you try to reach
this great speed at first, you will go over the
edge of the square, which is a fault in this exercise.   Yet it is better to do so now and then
than to draw the lines very slowly; for if you
do, the pen leaves a little dot of ink at the end
of each line, and these dots spoil your work.
So draw each line quickly, stopping always as
nearly as you can at the edge of the square.
The ends of lines which go over the edge are
afterwards to be removed with the penknife,
but not till you have done the whole work,

otherwise you roughen the paper, and the next
line that goes over the edge makes a blot.

9. When you have gone over the whole three
or four times, you will find some parts of the
square look darker than other parts.   Now try
to make the lighter parts as dark as the rest, so
that the whole may be of equal depth or darkness.   You will find, on examining the work,
that where it looks darkest the lines are closest,
or there are some much darker lines than elsewhere; therefore you must put in other lines,
or little scratches and dots, *between* the lines in
the paler parts; and where there are any very
conspicuous dark lines, scratch them out lightly
with the penknife, for the eye must not be
attracted by any line in particular.   The more
carefully and delicately you fill in the little gaps
and holes the better; you will get on faster by
doing two or three squares perfectly than a great
many badly.   As the tint gets closer and begins
to look even, work with very little ink in your
pen, so as hardly to make any mark on the paper;
and at last, where it is too dark, use the edge of
your penknife very lightly, and for some time, to
wear it softly into an even tone.   You will find
that the greatest difficulty consists in getting

evenness : one bit will always look darker than
another bit of your square ; or there will be
a granulated and sandy look over the whole.
When you find your paper quite rough and in
a mess, give it up and begin another square, but
do not rest satisfied till you have done your best
with every square.   The tint at last ought at
least to be as close and even as that in *b*, Fig. 1.
You will find, however, that it is very difficult to get a pale tint ; because, naturally, the
ink lines necessary to produce a close tint at all,
blacken the paper more than you want.   You
must get over this difficulty not so much by
leaving the lines wide apart as by trying to
draw them excessively fine, lightly and swiftly ;
being very cautious in filling in ; and, at last,
passing the penknife over the whole.   By keeping several squares in progress at one time, and
reserving your pen for the light one just when
the ink is nearly exhausted, you may get on
better.   The paper ought, at last, to look lightly
and evenly toned all over, with no lines distinctly visible.

EXERCISE II.

10. As this exercise in shading is very tire-
some, it will be well to vary it by proceeding
with another at the same time.   The power of
shading rightly depends mainly on lightness of
hand and keenness of sight; but there are other
qualities required in drawing, dependent not
merely on lightness, but steadiness of hand;
and the eye, to be perfect in its power, must
be made accurate as well as keen, and not only
see shrewdly, but measure justly.

11. Possess yourself therefore of any cheap
work on botany containing *outline* plates of
leaves and flowers, it does not matter whether
bad or good : Baxter's British Flowering Plants
is quite good enough.   Copy any of the simplest
outlines, first with a soft pencil, following it, by
the eye, as nearly as you can ; if it does not
look right in proportions, rub out and correct
it, always by the eye, till you think it is right :
when you have got it to your mind, lay tracing-
paper on the book; on this paper trace the outline you have been copying, and apply it to your
own ; and having thus ascertained the faults,
correct them all patiently, till you have got it

as nearly accurate as may be. Work with a
very soft pencil, and do not rub out so hard[1]
as to spoil the surface of your paper; never
mind how dirty the paper gets, but do not
roughen it; and let the false outlines alone
where they do not really interfere with the true
one. It is a good thing to accustom yourself
to hew and shape your drawing out of a dirty
piece of paper. When you have got it as right
as you can, take a quill pen, not very fine at
the point; rest your hand on a book about an
inch and a half thick, so as to hold the pen
long; and go over your pencil outline with ink,
raising your pen point as seldom as possible,
and never leaning more heavily on one part
of the line than on another. In most outline
drawings of the present day, parts of the curves

---

[1] Stale crumb of bread is better, if you are making a delicate
drawing, than India-rubber, for it disturbs the surface of the
paper less : but it crumbles about the room and makes a mess ;
and, besides, you waste the good bread, which is wrong ; and
your drawing will not for a long while be worth the crumbs.
So use India-rubber very lightly ; or, if heavily, pressing it
only, not passing it over the paper, and leave what pencil
marks will not come away so, without minding them. In a
finished drawing the uneffaced penciling is often serviceable,
helping the general tone, and enabling you to take out little
bright lights.

are thickened to give an effect of shade; all such outlines are bad, but they will serve well enough for your exercises, provided you do not imitate this character: it is better, however, if you can, to choose a book of pure outlines. It does not in the least matter whether your pen outline be thin or thick; but it matters greatly that it should be *equal*, not heavier in one place than in another. The power to be obtained is that of drawing an even line slowly and in any direction; all dashing lines, or approximations to penmanship, are bad. The pen should, as it were, walk slowly over the ground, and you should be able at any moment to stop it, or to turn it in any other direction, like a well-managed horse.

12. As soon as you can copy every curve *slowly* and accurately, you have made satisfactory progress; but you will find the difficulty is in the slowness. It is easy to draw what appears to be a good line with a sweep of the hand, or with what is called freedom;[1] the real

[1] What is usually so much sought after under the term "freedom" is the character of the drawing of a great master in a hurry, whose hand is so thoroughly disciplined, that when pressed for time he can let it fly as it will, and it will not go far wrong. But the hand of a great master at real *work*

difficulty and masterliness is in never letting the hand *be* free, but keeping it under entire control at every part of the line.

is *never* free : its swiftest dash is under perfect government. Paul Veronese or Tintoret could pause within a hair's breadth of any appointed mark, in their fastest touches ; and follow, within a hair's breadth, the previously intended curve. You must never, therefore, aim at freedom. It is not required of your drawing that it should be free, but that it should be right ; in time you will be able to do right easily, and then your work will be free in the best sense ; but there is no merit in doing wrong easily.

These remarks, however, do not apply to the lines used in shading, which, it will be remembered, are to be made as quickly as possible. The reason of this is, that the quicker a line is drawn, the lighter it is at the ends, and therefore the more easily joined with other lines, and concealed by them ; the object in perfect shading being to conceal the lines as much as possible.

And observe, in this exercise, the object is more to get firmness of hand than accuracy of eye for outline; for there are no outlines in Nature, and the ordinary student is sure to draw them falsely if he draws them at all. Do not, therefore, be discouraged if you find mistakes continue to occur in your outlines ; be content at present if you find your hand gaining command over the curves.

EXERCISE III.

13. Meantime, you are always to be going on with your shaded squares, and chiefly with these, the outline exercises being taken up only for rest.

As soon as you find you have some command of the pen as a shading instrument, and can lay a pale or dark tint as you choose, try to produce gradated spaces like Fig. 2, the dark

FIG. 2.

tint passing gradually into the lighter ones. Nearly all expression of form, in drawing, depends on your power of gradating delicately; and the gradation is always most skilful which passes from one tint into another very little paler. Draw, therefore, two parallel lines for limits to your work, as in Fig. 2, and try to gradate the shade evenly from white to black, passing over the greatest possible distance, yet so that every part of the band may have visible change in it.   The perception of gradation is very deficient in all beginners (not to say, in many artists), and you will probably, for some time, think your gradation skilful enough, when it is quite patchy and imperfect. By getting a piece of grey shaded riband, and comparing it with your drawing, you may arrive, in early stages of your work, at a wholesome dissatisfaction with it. Widen your band little by little as you get more skilful, so as to give the gradation more lateral space, and accustom yourself at the same time to look for gradated spaces in Nature. The sky is the largest and the most beautiful; watch it at twilight, after the sun is down, and try to consider each pane of glass in the window you look through as a piece of paper coloured blue, or grey, or purple, as it happens to be, and observe how quietly and continuously the gradation extends over the space in the window, of one or two feet square. Observe the shades on the outside and inside of a common white cup or bowl, which make it look round and hollow;[1] and then on folds of white drapery; and thus gradually you will be led to observe the more subtle transitions of the

[1] If you can get any pieces of dead white porcelain, not glazed, they will be useful models.

B

light as it increases or declines on flat surfaces. At last, when your eye gets keen and true, you will see gradation on everything in Nature.

14. But it will not be in your power yet awhile to draw from any objects in which the gradations are varied and complicated; nor will it be a bad omen for your future progress, and for the use that art is to be made of by you, if the first thing at which you aim should be a little bit of sky. So take any narrow space of evening sky, that you can usually see, between the boughs of a tree, or between two chimneys, or through the corner of a pane in the window you like best to sit at, and try to gradate a little space of white paper as evenly as that is gradated—as *tenderly* you cannot gradate it without colour, no, nor with colour either; but you may do it as evenly; or, if you get impatient with your spots and lines of ink, when you look at the beauty of the sky, the sense you will have gained of that beauty is something to be thankful for. But you ought not to be impatient with your pen and ink; for all great painters, however delicate their perception of

colour, are fond of the peculiar effect of light which may be got in a pen-and-ink sketch, and in a woodcut, by the gleaming of the white paper between the black lines; and if you cannot gradate well with pure black lines, you will never gradate well with pale ones. By looking at any common woodcuts, in the cheap publications of the day, you may see how gradation is given to the sky by leaving the lines farther and farther apart; but you must make your lines as fine as you can, as well as far apart, towards the light; and do not try to make them long or straight, but let them cross irregularly in any directions easy to your hand, depending on nothing but their gradation for your effect. On this point of direction of lines, however, I shall have to tell you more, presently; in the meantime, do not trouble yourself about it.

EXERCISE IV.

15. As soon as you find you can gradate
tolerably with the pen, take an H. or HH.
pencil, using its point to produce shade, from
the darkest possible to the palest, in exactly
the same manner as the pen, lightening, however, now with India-rubber instead of the
penknife.   You will find that all *pale* tints
of shade are thus easily producible with great
precision and tenderness, but that you cannot
get the same dark power as with the pen and
ink, and that the surface of the shade is apt
to become glossy and metallic, or dirty-looking,
or sandy.   Persevere, however, in trying to
bring it to evenness with the fine point, re-
moving any single speck or line that may
be too black, with the *point* of the knife : you
must not scratch the whole with the knife as
you do the ink.   If you find the texture very
speckled-looking, lighten it all over with India-
rubber, and recover it again with sharp, and
excessively fine touches of the pencil point,
bringing the parts that are too pale to perfect
evenness with the darker spots.

You cannot use the point too delicately or cunningly in doing this; work with it as if you were drawing the down on a butterfly's wing.

16. At this stage of your progress, if not before, you may be assured that some clever friend will come in, and hold up his hands in mocking amazement, and ask you who could set you to that "niggling;" and if you persevere in it, you will have to sustain considerable persecution from your artistical acquaintances generally, who will tell you that all good drawing depends on "boldness." But never mind them. You do not hear them tell a child, beginning music, to lay its little hand with a crash among the keys, in imitation of the great masters: yet they might, as reasonably as they may tell you to be bold in the present state of your knowledge. Bold, in the sense of being undaunted, yes; but bold in the sense of being careless, confident, or exhibitory,—no,—no, and a thousand times no; for, even if you were not a beginner, it would be bad advice that made you bold. Mischief may easily be done quickly, but good and beautiful work is generally done slowly;

you will find no boldness in the way a flower
or a bird's wing is painted; and if Nature
is not bold at her work, do you think you
ought to be at yours? So never mind what
people say, but work with your pencil point
very patiently; and if you can trust me in
anything, trust me when I tell you, that though
there are all kinds and ways of art,—large
work for large places, small work for narrow
places, slow work for people who can wait,
and quick work for people who cannot,—
there is one quality, and, I think, only one,
in which all great and good art agrees;—
it is all delicate art. Coarse art is always
bad art. You cannot understand this at
present, because you do not know yet how
much tender thought, and subtle care, the
great painters put into touches that at first
look coarse; but, believe me, it is true, and
you will find it is so in due time.

17. You will be perhaps also troubled, in
these first essays at pencil drawing, by noticing that more delicate gradations are got in an
instant by a chance touch of the India-rubber,
than by an hour's labour with the point; and
you may wonder why I tell you to produce

tints so painfully, which might, it appears, be
obtained with ease.   But there are two reasons :
the first, that when you come to draw forms,
you must be able to gradate with absolute
precision, in whatever place and direction you
wish ; not in any wise vaguely, as the India-
rubber does it : and, secondly, that all natural
shadows are more or less mingled with gleams
of light.   In the darkness of ground there is
the light of the little pebbles or dust; in the
darkness of foliage, the glitter of the leaves ;
in the darkness of flesh, transparency ; in
that of a stone, granulation : in every case
there is some mingling of light, which cannot
be represented by the leaden tone which you
get by rubbing, or by an instrument known to
artists as the "stump."   When you can manage the point properly, you will indeed be
able to do much also with this instrument,
or with your fingers ; but then you will have
to retouch the flat tints afterwards, so as to
put life and light into them, and that can
only be done with the point.   Labour on,
therefore, courageously, with that only.

EXERCISE V.

18. When you can manage to tint and gradate tenderly with the pencil point, get a good
large alphabet, and try to *tint* the letters into
shape with the pencil point. Do not outline
them first, but measure their height and ex-

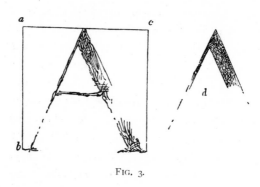

FIG. 3.

treme breadth with the compasses, as *a b*, *a c*,
Fig. 3, and then scratch in their shapes gradually; the letter A, enclosed within the lines,
being in what Turner would have called a
"state of forwardness." Then, when you are
satisfied with the shape of the letter, draw
pen-and-ink lines firmly round the tint, as

at *d*, and remove any touches outside the limit, first with the India-rubber, and then with the penknife, so that all may look clear and right. If you rub out any of the pencil inside the outline of the letter, retouch it, closing it up to the inked line. The straight lines of the outline are all to be ruled,[1] but the curved lines are to be drawn by the eye and hand; and you will soon find what good practice there is in getting the curved letters, such as Bs, Cs, &c., to stand quite straight, and come into accurate form.

19. All these exercises are very irksome, and they are not to be persisted in alone; neither is it necessary to acquire perfect power in any of them. An entire master of the

---

[1] Artists who glance at this book may be surprised at this permission. My chief reason is, that I think it more necessary that the pupil's eye should be trained to accurate perception of the relations of curve and right lines, by having the latter absolutely true, than that he should practise drawing straight lines. But also, I believe, though I am not quite sure of this, that he never *ought* to be able to draw a straight line. I do not believe a perfectly trained hand ever can draw a line without some curvature in it, or some variety of direction. Prout could draw a straight line, but I do not believe Raphael could, nor Tintoret. A great draughtsman can, as far as I have observed, draw every line *but* a straight one.

pencil or brush ought, indeed, to be able to
draw any form at once, as Giotto his circle;
but such skill as this is only to be expected
of the consummate master, having pencil in
hand all his life, and all day long,—hence the
force of Giotto's proof of his skill; and it is
quite possible to draw very beautifully, without attaining even an approximation to such
a power; the main point being, not that every
line should be precisely what we intend or
wish, but that the line which we intended or
wished to draw should be right.   If we always
see rightly and mean rightly, we shall get on,
though the hand may stagger a little; but if
we mean wrongly, or mean nothing, it does
not matter how firm the hand is.   Do not
therefore torment yourself because you cannot do as well as you would like; but work
patiently, sure that every square and letter
will give you a certain increase of power; and
as soon as you can draw your letters pretty
well, here is a more amusing exercise for
you.

EXERCISE VI.

20. Choose any tree that you think pretty, which is nearly bare of leaves, and which you can see against the sky, or against a pale wall, or other light ground: it must not be against strong light, or you will find the looking at it hurt your eyes; nor must it be in sunshine, or you will be puzzled by the lights on the boughs. But the tree must be in shade; and the sky blue, or grey, or dull white. A wholly grey or rainy day is the best for this practice.

21. You will see that all the boughs of the tree are dark against the sky. Consider them as so many dark rivers, to be laid down in a map with absolute accuracy; and, without the least thought about the roundness of the stems, map them all out in flat shade, scrawling them in with pencil, just as you did the limbs of your letters; then correct and alter them, rubbing out and out again, never minding how much your paper is dirtied (only not destroying its surface), until every bough is exactly, or as near as your utmost power can bring it, right in curvature and in thickness. Look at the

white interstices between them with as much
scrupulousness as if they were little estates
which you had to survey, and draw maps of,
for some important lawsuit, involving heavy
penalties if you cut the least bit of a corner off
any of them, or gave the hedge anywhere too
deep a curve ; and try continually to fancy the
whole tree nothing but a flat ramification on a
white ground.   Do not take any trouble about
the little twigs, which look like a confused network or mist; leave them all out,[1] drawing
only the main branches as far as you can see
them distinctly, your object at present being
not to draw a tree, but to learn how to do so.
When you have got the thing as nearly right
as you can,—and it is better to make one good
study, than twenty left unnecessarily inaccurate,
—take your pen, and put a fine outline to all
the boughs, as you did to your letter, taking
care, as far as possible, to put the outline within the edge of the shade, so as not to make the
boughs thicker : the main use of the outline is

---

[1] Or, if you feel able to do so, scratch them in with confused
quick touches, indicating the general shape of the cloud or
mist of twigs round the main branches ; but do not take much
trouble about them.

to affirm the whole more clearly; to do away
with little accidental roughnesses and excres-
cences, and especially to mark where boughs
cross, or come in front of each other, as at such

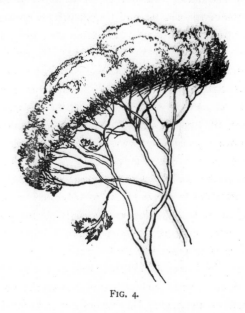

FIG. 4.

points their arrangement in this kind of sketch
is unintelligible without the outline. It may
perfectly well happen that in Nature it should
be less distinct than your outline will make it;

but it is better in this kind of sketch to mark
the facts clearly.   The temptation is always to
be slovenly and careless, and the outline is like
a bridle, and forces our indolence into attention
and precision.   The outline should be about
the thickness of that in Fig. 4, which represents
the ramification of a small stone pine, only I
have not endeavoured to represent the pencil
shading within the outline, as I could not easily
express it in a woodcut ; and you have nothing
to do at present with the indication of foliage
above, of which in another place.   You may
also draw your trees as much larger than this
figure as you like ; only, however large they
may be, keep the outline as delicate, and draw
the branches far enough into their outer sprays
to give quite as slender ramification as you
have in this figure, otherwise you do not get
good enough practice out of them.

22. You cannot do too many studies of
this kind : every one will give you some new
notion about trees.   But when you are tired
of tree boughs, take any forms whatever which
are drawn in flat colour, one upon another ;
as patterns on any kind of cloth, or flat china
(tiles, for instance), executed in two colours

only; and practise drawing them of the right shape and size by the eye, and filling them in with shade of the depth required.

In doing this, you will first have to meet the difficulty of representing depth of colour by depth of shade. Thus a pattern of ultramarine blue will have to be represented by a darker tint of grey than a pattern of yellow.

23. And now it is both time for you to begin to learn the mechanical use of the brush; and necessary for you to do so in order to provide yourself with the gradated scale of colour which you will want. If you can, by any means, get acquainted with any ordinary skilful water-colour painter, and prevail on him to show you how to lay on tints with a brush, by all means do so; not that you are yet, nor for a long while yet, to begin to colour, but because the brush is often more convenient than the pencil for laying on masses or tints of shade, and the sooner you know how to manage it as an instrument the better. If, however, you have no opportunity of seeing how water-colour is laid on by a workman of any kind, the following directions will help you :—

EXERCISE VII.

24. Get a shilling cake of Prussian blue.
Dip the end of it in water so as to take up
a drop, and rub it in a white saucer till you
cannot rub much more, and the colour gets
dark, thick, and oily-looking.   Put two teaspoonfuls of water to the colour you have
rubbed down, and mix it well up with a
camel's-hair brush about three quarters of an
inch long.

25. Then take a piece of smooth, but not
glossy, Bristol board or pasteboard; divide
it, with your pencil and rule, into squares
as large as those of the very largest chess-
board: they need not be perfect squares, only
as nearly so as you can quickly guess.   Rest
the pasteboard on something sloping as much
as an ordinary desk; then, dipping your brush
into the colour you have mixed, and taking
up as much of the liquid as it will carry,
begin at the top of one of the squares, and
lay a pond or runlet of colour along the
top edge.   Lead this pond of colour gradually downwards, not faster at one place than

another, but as if you were adding a row of
bricks to a building, all along (only building
down instead of up), dipping the brush frequently so as to keep the colour as full in
that, and in as great quantity on the paper,
as you can, so only that it does not run
down anywhere in a little stream.   But if it
should, never mind; go on quietly with your
square till you have covered it all in.   When
you get to the bottom, the colour will lodge
there in a great wave.   Have ready a piece
of blotting-paper; dry your brush on it, and
with the dry brush take up the superfluous
colour as you would with a sponge, till it all
looks even.

26. In leading the colour down, you will
find your brush continually go over the edge
of the square, or leave little gaps within it.
Do not endeavour to retouch these, nor take
much care about them; the great thing is to
get the colour to lie smoothly where it reaches,
not in alternate blots and pale patches; try,
therefore, to lead it over the square as fast
as possible, with such attention to your limit
as you are able to give.   The use of the
exercise is, indeed, to enable you finally to

c

strike the colour up to the limit with perfect
accuracy; but the first thing is to get it
even,—the power of rightly striking the edge
comes only by time and practice: even the
greatest artists rarely can do this quite perfectly.

27. When you have done one square, proceed
to do another which does not communicate with
it.   When you have thus done all the alternate
squares, as on a chess-board, turn the pasteboard upside down, begin again with the first,
and put another coat over it, and so on over
all the others.   The use of turning the paper
upside down is to neutralise the increase of
darkness towards the bottom of the squares,
which would otherwise take place from the
ponding of the colour.

28. Be resolved to use blotting-paper, or a
piece of rag, instead of your lips, to dry the
brush.   The habit of doing so, once acquired,
will save you from much partial poisoning.
Take care, however, always to draw the brush
from root to point, otherwise you will spoil it.
You may even wipe it as you would a pen
when you want it very dry, without doing
harm, provided you do not crush it upwards.

Get a good brush at first, and cherish it; it will serve you longer and better than many bad ones.

29. When you have done the squares all over again, do them a third time, always trying to keep your edges as neat as possible. When your colour is exhausted, mix more in the same proportions, two teaspoonfuls to as much as you can grind with a drop; and when you have done the alternate squares three times over, as the paper will be getting very damp, and dry more slowly, begin on the white squares, and bring them up to the same tint in the same way. The amount of jagged dark line which then will mark the limits of the squares will be the exact measure of your unskilfulness.

30. As soon as you tire of squares draw circles (with compasses); and then draw straight lines irregularly across circles, and fill up the spaces so produced between the straight line and the circumference; and then draw any simple shapes of leaves, according to the exercise No. II., and fill up those, until you can lay on colour quite evenly in any shape you want.

31. You will find in the course of this

practice, as you cannot always put exactly
the same quantity of water to the colour,
that the darker the colour is, the more difficult it becomes to lay it on evenly. Therefore, when you have gained some definite
degree of power, try to fill in the forms required with a full brush, and a dark tint,
at once, instead of laying several coats one
over another; always taking care that the
tint, however dark, be quite liquid; and that,
after being laid on, so much of it is absorbed
as to prevent its forming a black line at the
edge as it dries. A little experience will teach
you how apt the colour is to do this, and how
to prevent it; not that it needs always to be
prevented, for a great master in water-colours
will sometimes draw a firm outline, when he
wants one, simply by letting the colour dry
in this way at the edge.

32. When, however, you begin to cover
complicated forms with the darker colour, no
rapidity will prevent the tint from drying
irregularly as it is led on from part to part.
You will then find the following method useful. Lay in the colour very pale and liquid;
so pale, indeed, that you can only just see

where it is on the paper. Lead it up to **all the** outlines, and make it precise in form, keeping it thoroughly wet everywhere. Then, when it is all in shape, take the darker colour, and lay some of it *into* the middle of the liquid colour. It will spread gradually in a branchy kind of way, and you may now lead it up to the outlines already determined, and play it with the brush till it fills its place well; then let it dry, and it will be as flat and pure as a single dash, yet defining all the complicated forms accurately.

33. Having thus obtained the power of laying on a tolerably flat tint, you must try to lay on a gradated one. Prepare the colour with three or four teaspoonfuls of water; then, when it is mixed, pour away about two thirds of it, keeping a teaspoonful of pale colour. Sloping your paper as before, draw two pencil lines all the way down, leaving a space between them of the width of a square on your chess-board. Begin at the top of your paper, between the lines; and having struck on the first brushful of colour, and led it down a little, dip your brush deep in water, and mix up the colour on the plate quickly with as much more water

as the brush takes up at that one dip: then, with this paler colour, lead the tint farther down.   Dip in water again, mix the colour again, and thus lead down the tint, always dipping in water once between each replenishing of the brush, and stirring the colour on the plate well, but as quickly as you can.   Go on until the colour has become so pale that you cannot see it; then wash your brush thoroughly in water, and carry the wave down a little farther with that, and then absorb it with the dry brush, and leave it to dry.

34. If you get to the bottom of your paper before your colour gets pale, you may either take longer paper, or begin, with the tint as it was when you left off, on another sheet; but be sure to exhaust it to pure whiteness at last.   When all is quite dry, recommence at the top with another similar mixture of colour, and go down in the same way.   Then again, and then again, and so continually until the colour at the top of the paper is as dark as your cake of Prussian blue, and passes down into pure white paper at the end of your column, with a perfectly smooth gradation from one into the other.

35. You will find at first that the paper gets mottled or wavy, instead of evenly gradated; this is because at some places you have taken up more water in your brush than at others, or not mixed it thoroughly on the plate, or led one tint too far before replenishing with the next. Practice only will enable you to do it well; the best artists cannot always get gradations of this kind quite to their minds; nor do they ever leave them on their pictures without after-touching.

36. As you get more power, and can strike the colour more quickly down, you will be able to gradate in less compass;[1] beginning with a small quantity of colour, and adding a drop of water, instead of a brushful; with finer brushes, also, you may gradate to a less scale. But slight skill will enable you to test the relations of colour to shade as far as is necessary for your immediate progress, which is to be done thus :—

37. Take cakes of lake, of gamboge, of sepia, of blue-black, of cobalt, and vermilion; and

---

[1] It is more difficult, at first, to get, in colour, a narrow gradation than an extended one; but the ultimate difficulty is, as with the pen, to make the gradation go *far*.

prepare gradated columns (exactly as you
have done with the Prussian blue) of the
lake and blue-black.[1] Cut a narrow slip, all
the way down, of each gradated colour, and
set the three slips side by side; fasten them
down, and rule lines at equal distances across
all the three, so as to divide them into fifty
degrees, and number the degrees of each, from
light to dark, 1, 2, 3, &c. If you have gradated them rightly, the darkest part either of
the red or blue will be nearly equal in power
to the darkest part of the blue-black, and any
degree of the black slip will also, accurately
enough for our purpose, balance in weight the
degree similarly numbered in the red or the
blue slip. Then, when you are drawing from
objects of a crimson or blue colour, if you can
match their colour by any compartment of the
crimson or blue in your scales, the grey in the
compartment of the grey scale marked with the
same number is the grey which must represent
that crimson or blue in your light and shade
drawing.

38. Next, prepare scales with gamboge,

[1] Of course, all the columns of colour are to be of equal
length.

cobalt, and vermilion. You will find that you cannot darken these beyond a certain point;[1] for yellow and scarlet, so long as they remain yellow and scarlet, cannot approach to black; we cannot have, properly speaking, a dark yellow or dark scarlet. Make your scales of full yellow, blue, and scarlet, half-way down; passing *then* gradually to white. Afterwards use lake to darken the upper half of the vermilion and gamboge; and Prussian blue to darken the cobalt. You will thus have three more scales, passing from white nearly to black, through yellow and orange, through sky-blue, and through scarlet. By mixing the gamboge and Prussian blue you may make another with green; mixing the cobalt and lake, another with violet; the sepia alone will make a forcible brown one; and so on, until you have as many scales as you like, passing from black to white through different colours. Then, supposing your scales properly gradated and equally divided, the compartment or degree No. I

---

[1] The degree of darkness you can reach with the given colour is always indicated by the colour of the solid cake in the box.

of the grey will represent in chiaroscuro the
No. 1 of all the other colours; No. 2 of grey
the No. 2 of the other colours, and so on.

39. It is only necessary, however, in this
matter that you should understand the principle; for it would never be possible for you
to gradate your scales so truly as to make
them practically accurate and serviceable; and
even if you could, unless you had about ten
thousand scales, and were able to change them
faster than ever juggler changed cards, you
could not in a day measure the tints on so
much as one side of a frost-bitten apple. But
when once you fully understand the principle,
and see how all colours contain as it were a
certain quantity of darkness, or power of dark
relief from white—some more, some less; and
how this pitch or power of each may be represented by equivalent values of grey, you
will soon be able to arrive shrewdly at an
approximation by a glance of the eye, without
any measuring scale at all.

40. You must now go on, again with the
pen, drawing patterns, and any shapes of shade
that you think pretty, as veinings in marble
or tortoiseshell, spots in surfaces of shells,

&c., as tenderly as you can, in the darknesses that correspond to their colours; and when you find you can do this successfully, it is time to begin rounding.

EXERCISE VIII.

41. Go out into your garden, or into the road, and pick up the first round or oval stone you can find, not very white, nor very dark; and the smoother it is the better, only it must not *shine*. Draw your table near the window, and put the stone, which I will suppose is about the size of *a* in Fig. 5 (it had better not be much larger), on a piece of not very white paper, on the table in front of you. Sit so that the light may come from your left, else the shadow of the pencil point interferes with your sight of your work. You must not let the *sun* fall on the stone, but only ordinary light: therefore choose a window which the sun does not come in at. If you can shut the shutters of the other windows in the room it will be all the better; but this is not of much consequence.

42. Now if you can draw that stone, you

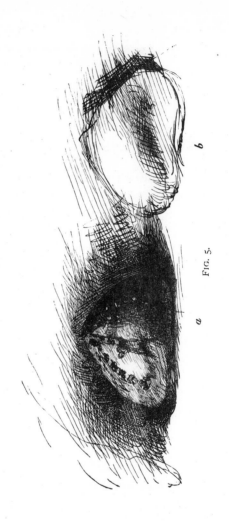

b

a

FIG. 5.

can draw anything; I mean, anything that is drawable. Many things (sea foam, for instance) cannot be drawn at all, only the idea of them more or less suggested; but if you can draw the stone *rightly*, everything within reach of art is also within yours.

For all drawing depends, primarily, on your power of representing *Roundness*. If you can once do that, all the rest is easy and straightforward; if you cannot do that, nothing else that you may be able to do will be of any use. For Nature is all made up of roundnesses; not the roundness of perfect globes, but of variously curved surfaces. Boughs are rounded, leaves are rounded, stones are rounded, clouds are rounded, cheeks are rounded, and curls are rounded: there is no more flatness in the natural world than there is vacancy. The world itself is round, and so is all that is in it, more or less, except human work, which is often very flat indeed.

Therefore, set yourself steadily to conquer that round stone, and you have won the battle.

43. Look your stone antagonist boldly in the face. You will see that the side of it

next the window is lighter than most of the
paper; that the side of it farthest from the
window is darker than the paper; and that
the light passes into the dark gradually, while
a shadow is thrown to the right on the paper
itself by the stone: the general appearance
of things being more or less as in *a*, Fig. 5,
the spots on the stone excepted, of which
more presently.

44. Now, remember always what was stated
in the outset, that everything you can see in
Nature is seen only so far as it is lighter
or darker than the things about it, or of a
different colour from them. It is either seen
as a patch of one colour on a ground of
another; or as a pale thing relieved from a
dark thing, or a dark thing from a pale thing.
And if you can put on patches of colour or
shade of exactly the same size, shape, and
gradations as those on the object and its
ground, you will produce the appearance of
the object and its ground. The best draughtsman—Titian and Paul Veronese themselves—
could do no more than this; and you will
soon be able to get some power of doing it
in an inferior way, if you once understand

the exceeding simplicity of what is to be done.
Suppose you have a brown book on a white
sheet of paper, on a red tablecloth. You have
nothing to do but to put on spaces of red,
white, and brown, in the same shape, and
gradated from dark to light in the same degrees, and your drawing is done. If you will
not look at what you see, if you try to put on
brighter or duller colours than are there, if
you try to put them on with a dash or a blot,
or to cover your paper with "vigorous" lines,
or to produce anything, in fact, but the plain,
unaffected, and finished tranquillity of the thing
before you, you need not hope to get on.
Nature will show you nothing if you set yourself up for her master. But forget yourself,
and try to obey her, and you will find obedience
easier and happier than you think.

45. The real difficulties are to get the refinement of the forms and the evenness of
the gradations. You may depend upon it,
when you are dissatisfied with your work,
it is always too coarse or too uneven. It
may not be wrong—in all probability is not
wrong, in any (so-called) great point. But
its edges are not true enough in outline;

and its shades are in blotches, or scratches, or full of white holes. Get it more tender and more true, and you will find it is more powerful.

46. Do not, therefore, think your drawing must be weak because you have a finely pointed pen in your hand. Till you can draw with that, you can draw with nothing; when you can draw with that, you can draw with a log of wood charred at the end. True boldness and power are only to be gained by care. Even in fencing and dancing, all ultimate ease depends on early precision in the commencement; much more in singing or drawing.

47. Now I do not want you to copy my sketch in Fig. 5, but to copy the stone before you in the way that my sketch is done. To which end, first measure the extreme length of the stone with compasses, and mark that length on your paper; then, between the points marked, leave something like the form of the stone in light, scrawling the paper all over, round it; *b*, in Fig. 5, is a beginning of this kind. Rather leave too much room for the high light, than too little; and then

more cautiously fill in the shade, shutting
the light gradually up, and putting in the
dark slowly on the dark side. You need
not plague yourself about accuracy of shape,
because, till you have practised a great deal,
it is impossible for you to draw the shape of
the stone quite truly, and you must gradually
gain correctness by means of these various
exercises: what you have mainly to do at
present is, to get the stone to look solid
and round, not much minding what its exact
contour is—only draw it as nearly right as
you can without vexation; and you will get
it more right by thus feeling your way to
it in shade, than if you tried to draw the
outline at first. For you can *see* no outline; what you see is only a certain space
of gradated shade, with other such spaces
about it; and those pieces of shade you are
to imitate as nearly as you can, by scrawling
the paper over till you get them to the right
shape, with the same gradations which they
have in Nature. And this is really more
likely to be done well, if you have to fight
your way through a little confusion in the
sketch, than if you have an accurately traced

D

outline. For instance, having sketched the fossil sea-urchin at *a*, in Fig. 5, whose form, though irregular, required more care in following than that of a common stone, I was going to draw it also under another effect; reflected light bringing its dark side out from the background: but when I had laid on the first few touches I thought it would be better to stop, and let you see how I had begun it, at *b*. In which beginning it will be observed that nothing is so determined but that I can more or less modify, and add to or diminish the contour as I work on, the lines which suggest the outline being blended with the others if I do not want them; and the having to fill up the vacancies and conquer the irregularities of such a sketch will probably secure a higher completion at last, than if half an hour had been spent in getting a true outline before beginning.

48. In doing this, however, take care not to get the drawing too dark. In order to ascertain what the shades of it really are, cut a round hole, about half the size of a pea, in a piece of white paper the colour of that you use to draw on. Hold this bit of paper with

the hole in it, between you and your stone;
and pass the paper backwards and forwards,
so as to see the different portions of the stone
(or other subject) through the hole.   You will
find that, thus, the circular hole looks like one
of the patches of colour you have been accustomed to match, only changing in depth as it
lets different pieces of the stone be seen through
it.   You will be able thus actually to *match* the
colour of the stone at any part of it, by tinting
the paper beside the circular opening.   And
you will find that this opening never looks
quite *black*, but that all the roundings of the
stone are given by subdued greys.[1]

49. You will probably find, also, that some
parts of the stone, or of the paper it lies on,
look luminous through the opening; so that
the little circle then tells as a light spot instead of a dark spot.   When this is so, you
cannot imitate it, for you have no means of
getting light brighter than white paper: but
by holding the paper more sloped towards the
light, you will find that many parts of the

---

[1] The figure *a*, Fig. 5, is very dark, but this is to give an
example of all kinds of depths of tint, without repeated
figures.

stone, which before looked light through the
hole, then look dark through it; and if you
can place the paper in such a position that
every part of the stone looks slightly dark,
the little hole will tell always as a spot of
shade, and if your drawing is put in the same
light, you can imitate or match every gradation. You will be amazed to find, under
these circumstances, how slight the differences
of tint are, by which, through infinite delicacy
of gradation, Nature can express form.

If any part of your subject will obstinately
show itself as a light through the hole, that
part you need not hope to imitate. Leave it
white; you can do no more.

50. When you have done the best you can
to get the general form, proceed to finish, by
imitating the texture and all the cracks and
stains of the stone as closely as you can; and
note, in doing this, that cracks or fissures of
any kind, whether between stones in walls,
or in the grain of timber or rocks, or in any
of the thousand other conditions they present,
are never expressible by single black lines, or
lines of simple shadow. A crack must always
have its complete system of light and shade,

however small its scale. It is in reality a little ravine, with a dark or shady side, and light or sunny side, and, usually, shadow in the bottom. This is one of the instances in which it may be as well to understand the reason of the appearance; it is not often so in drawing, for the aspects of things are so subtle and confused that they cannot in general be explained; and in the endeavour to explain some, we are sure to lose sight of others, while the natural over-estimate of the importance of those on which the attention is fixed causes us to exaggerate them, so that merely scientific draughtsmen caricature a third part of Nature, and miss two thirds. The best scholar is he whose eye is so keen as to see at once how the thing looks, and who need not therefore trouble himself with any reasons why it looks so: but few people have this acuteness of perception; and to those who are destitute of it, a little pointing out of rule and reason will be a help, especially when a master is not near them. I never allow my own pupils to ask the reason of anything, because, as I watch their work, I can always show them how the thing IS, and what appearance they are missing in it ; but when a master is not by to direct the sight, science may, here and there, be allowed to do so in his stead.

51. Generally, then, every solid illumined object—for instance, the stone you are drawing —has a light side turned towards the light, a dark side turned away from the light, and a shadow, which is cast on something else (as by the stone on the paper it is set upon). You may sometimes be placed so as to see only the light side and shadow, sometimes only the dark side and shadow, and sometimes both or either without the shadow ; but in most positions solid objects will show all the three, as the stone does here.

52. Hold up your hand with the edge of it towards you, as you sit now with your side to the window, so that the flat of your hand is turned to the window. You will see one side of your hand distinctly lighted, the other distinctly in shade. Here are light side and dark side, with no seen shadow ; the shadow being detached, perhaps on the table, perhaps on the other side of the room ; you need not look for it at present.

53. Take a sheet of note-paper, and holding it edgewise, as you hold your hand, wave it

up and down past the side of your hand which
is turned from the light, the paper being of
course farther from the window. You will
see, as it passes, a strong gleam of light strike
on your hand, and light it considerably on its
dark side. This light is *reflected* light. It is
thrown back from the paper (on which it
strikes first in coming from the window) to
the surface of your hand, just as a ball would
be if somebody threw it through the window
at the wall and you caught it at the rebound.

Next, instead of the note-paper, take a red
book, or a piece of scarlet cloth. You will see
that the gleam of light falling on your hand,
as you wave the book, is now reddened. Take
a blue book, and you will find the gleam is
blue. Thus every object will cast some of its
own colour back in the light that it reflects.

54. Now it is not only these books or papers
that reflect light to your hand: every object
in the room on that side of it reflects some,
but more feebly, and the colours mixing all
together form a neutral[1] light, which lets the

---

[1] Nearly neutral in ordinary circumstances, but yet with
quite different tones in its neutrality, according to the colours
of the various reflected rays that compose it.

colour of your hand itself be more distinctly
seen than that of any object which reflects
light to it; but if there were no reflected light,
that side of your hand would look as black as
a coal.

55. Objects are seen therefore, in general,
partly by direct light, and partly by light reflected from the objects around them, or from
the atmosphere and clouds. The colour of
their light sides depends much on that of the
direct light, and that of the dark sides on the
colours of the objects near them. It is therefore impossible to say beforehand what colour
an object will have at any point of its surface,
that colour depending partly on its own tint,
and partly on infinite combinations of rays
reflected from other things. The only certain
fact about dark sides is, that their colour will
be changeful, and that a picture which gives
them merely darker shades of the colour of
the light sides must assuredly be bad.

56. Now, lay your hand flat on the white
paper you are drawing on. You will see one
side of each finger lighted, one side dark, and
the shadow of your hand on the paper. Here,
therefore, are the three divisions of shade seen

at once. And although the paper is white, and
your hand of a rosy colour somewhat darker
than white, yet you will see that the shadow
all along, just under the finger which casts it,
is darker than the flesh, and is of a very deep
grey. The reason of this is, that much light
is reflected from the paper to the dark side of
your finger, but very little is reflected from
other things to the paper itself in that chink
under your finger.

57. In general, for this reason, a shadow,
or, at any rate, the part of the shadow nearest
the object, is darker than the dark side of the
object. I say in general, because a thousand
accidents may interfere to prevent its being
so. Take a little bit of glass, as a wine-glass,
or the ink-bottle, and play it about a little
on the side of your hand farthest from the
window; you will presently find you are
throwing gleams of light all over the dark
side of your hand, and in some positions of
the glass the reflection from it will annihilate
the shadow altogether, and you will see your
hand dark on the white paper. Now a
stupid painter would represent, for instance,
a drinking-glass beside the hand of one of

his figures, and because he had been taught by rule that "shadow was darker than the dark side," he would never think of the reflection from the glass, but paint a dark grey under the hand, just as if no glass were there. But a great painter would be sure to think of the true effect, and paint it; and then comes the stupid critic, and wonders why the hand is so light on its dark side.

58. Thus it is always dangerous to assert anything as a *rule* in matters of art; yet it is useful for you to remember that, in a general way, a shadow is darker than the dark side of the thing that casts it, supposing the colours otherwise the same; that is to say, when a white object casts a shadow on a white surface, or a dark object on a dark surface: the rule will not hold if the colours are different, the shadow of a black object on a white surface being, of course, not so dark, usually, as the black thing casting it. The only way to ascertain the ultimate truth in such matters is to *look* for it; but, in the meantime, you will be helped by noticing that the cracks in the stone are little ravines, on one side of which the light strikes sharply,

while the other is in shade. This dark side
usually casts a little darker shadow at the
bottom of the crack; and the general tone
of the stone surface is not so bright as the
light bank of the ravine. And, therefore,
if you get the surface of the object of a
uniform tint, more or less indicative of shade,
and then scratch out a white spot or streak
in it of any shape; by putting a dark touch
beside this white one, you may turn it, as
you choose, into either a ridge or an incision,
into either a boss or a cavity. If you put
the dark touch on the side of it nearest the
sun, or rather, nearest the place that the
light comes from, you will make it a cut or
cavity; if you put it on the opposite side,
you will make it a ridge or mound; and
the complete success of the effect depends
less on depth of shade than on the rightness
of the drawing; that is to say, on the evident
correspondence of the form of the shadow
with the form that casts it. In drawing
rocks, or wood, or anything irregularly shaped,
you will gain far more by a little patience in
following the forms carefully, though with
slight touches, than by laboured finishing of

texture of surface and transparencies of
shadow.

59. When you have got the whole well
into shape, proceed to lay on the stains and
spots with great care, quite as much as you
gave to the forms. Very often, spots or
bars of local colour do more to express form
than even the light and shade, and they are
always interesting as the means by which
Nature carries light into her shadows, and
shade into her lights; an art of which we
shall have more to say hereafter, in speaking
of composition. *a*, in Fig. 5, is a rough
sketch of a fossil sea-urchin, in which the
projections of the shell are of black flint,
coming through a chalky surface. These
projections form dark spots in the light; and
their sides, rising out of the shadow, form
smaller whiter spots in the dark. You may
take such scattered lights as these out with
the penknife, provided you are just as careful
to place them rightly as if you got them by
a more laborious process.

60. When you have once got the feeling
of the way in which gradation expresses
roundness and projection, you may try your

strength on anything natural or artificial that
happens to take your fancy, provided it be
not too complicated in form. I have asked
you to draw a stone first, because any irregularities and failures in your shading will
be less offensive to you, as being partly
characteristic of the rough stone surface, than
they would be in a more delicate subject ;
and you may as well go on drawing rounded
stones of different shapes for a little while,
till you find you can really shade delicately.
You may then take up folds of thick white
drapery, a napkin or towel thrown carelessly
on the table is as good as anything, and try
to express them in the same way ; only now
you will find that your shades must be
wrought with perfect unity and tenderness,
or you will lose the flow of the folds. Always
remember that a little bit perfected is worth
more than many scrawls ; whenever you feel
yourself inclined to scrawl, give up work
resolutely, and do not go back to it till next
day. Of course your towel or napkin must
be put on something that may be locked up,
so that its folds shall not be disturbed till
you have finished. If you find that the folds

will not look right, get a photograph of a
piece of drapery (there are plenty now to
be bought, taken from the sculpture of the
cathedrals of Rheims, Amiens, and Chartres,
which will at once educate your hand and
your taste), and copy some piece of that;
you will then ascertain what it is that is
wanting in your studies from Nature, whether
more gradation, or greater watchfulness of
the disposition of the folds. Probably for
some time you will find yourself failing painfully in both, for drapery is very difficult to
follow in its sweeps; but do not lose courage,
for the greater the difficulty, the greater the
gain in the effort. If your eye is more
just in measurement of form than delicate
in perception of tint, a pattern on the folded
surface will help you. Try whether it does
or not: and if the patterned drapery confuses
you, keep for a time to the simple white
one; but if it helps you, continue to choose
patterned stuffs (tartans and simple chequered
designs are better at first than flowered ones),
and even though it should confuse you, begin
pretty soon to use a pattern occasionally,
copying all the distortions and perspective

modifications of it among the folds with scrupulous care.

61. Neither must you suppose yourself condescending in doing this. The greatest masters are always fond of drawing patterns; and the greater they are, the more pains they take to do it truly.[1] Nor can there be better practice at any time, as introductory to the nobler complication of natural detail. For when you can draw the spots which follow the folds of a printed stuff, you will have some chance of following the spots which fall into the folds of the skin of a leopard as he leaps; but if you cannot draw the manufacture, assuredly you will never be able to draw the creature. So the cloudings on a piece of wood, carefully drawn, will be the best introduction to the drawing of the clouds of the sky, or the waves of the sea; and the dead leaf-patterns on a

---

[1] If we had any business with the reasons of this, I might perhaps be able to show you some metaphysical ones for the enjoyment, by truly artistical minds, of the changes wrought by light and shade and perspective in patterned surfaces; but this is at present not to the point; and all that you need to know is that the drawing of such things is good exercise, and moreover a kind of exercise which Titian, Veronese, Tintoret, Giorgione, and Turner, all enjoyed, and strove to excel in.

damask drapery, well rendered, will enable
you to disentangle masterfully the living leaf-
patterns of a thorn thicket or a violet bank.

62. Observe, however, in drawing any stuffs,
or bindings of books, or other finely textured
substances, do not trouble yourself, as yet,
much about the woolliness or gauziness of
the thing; but get it right in shade and fold,
and true in pattern. We shall see, in the
course of after-practice, how the penned lines
may be made indicative of texture; but at
present attend only to the light and shade
and pattern. You will be puzzled at first
by *lustrous* surfaces, but a little attention will
show you that the expression of these depends
merely on the right drawing of their light
and shade, and reflections. Put a small
black japanned tray on the table in front of
some books; and you will see it reflects the
objects beyond it as in a little black rippled
pond; its own colour mingling always with
that of the reflected objects. Draw these reflections of the books properly, making them
dark and distorted, as you will see that they
are, and you will find that this gives the
lustre to your tray. It is not well, however,

to draw polished objects in general practice; only you should do one or two in order to understand the aspect of any lustrous portion of other things, such as you cannot avoid; the gold, for instance, on the edges of books, or the shining of silk and damask, in which lies a great part of the expression of their folds.   Observe also that there are very few things which are totally without lustre; you will frequently find a light which puzzles you, on some apparently dull surface, to be the dim image of another object.

63. And now, as soon as you can conscientiously assure me that with the point of the pen or pencil you can lay on any form and shade you like, I give you leave to use the brush with one colour,—sepia, or blue black, or mixed cobalt and blue black, or neutral tint; and this will much facilitate your study, and refresh you. But, preliminary, you must do one or two more exercises in tinting.

E

EXERCISE IX.

64. Prepare your colour as directed for Exercise VII. Take a brush full of it, and strike it on the paper in any irregular shape; as the brush gets dry, sweep the surface of the paper with it as if you were dusting the paper very lightly; every such sweep of the brush will leave a number of more or less minute interstices in the colour. The lighter and faster every dash the better. Then leave the whole to dry; and, as soon as it is dry, with little colour in your brush, so that you can bring it to a fine point, fill up all the little interstices one by one, so as to make the whole as even as you can, and fill in the larger gaps with more colour, always trying to let the edges of the first and of the newly applied colour exactly meet, and not lap over each other. When your new colour dries, you will find it in places a little paler than the first. Retouch it therefore, trying to get the whole to look quite one piece. A very small bit of colour thus filled up with your very best care, and brought to look as if it had been

quite even from the first, will give you better practice and more skill than a great deal filled in carelessly ; so do it with your best patience, not leaving the most minute spot of white ; and do not fill in the large pieces first and then go to the small, but quietly and steadily cover in the whole up to a marked limit; then advance a little farther, and so on ; thus always seeing distinctly what is done and what undone.

EXERCISE X.

65. Lay a coat of the blue, prepared as usual, over a whole square of paper. Let it dry. Then another coat over four fifths of the square, or thereabouts, leaving the edge rather irregular than straight, and let it dry. Then another coat over three fifths; another over two fifths; and the last over one fifth ; so that the square may present the appearance of gradual increase in darkness in five bands, each darker than the one beyond it. Then, with the brush rather dry (as in the former exercise, when filling up the interstices), try,

with small touches, like those used in the
pen etching, only a little broader, to add shade
delicately beyond each edge, so as to lead
the darker tints into the paler ones imper-
ceptibly. By touching the paper very lightly,
and putting a multitude of little touches,
crossing and recrossing in every direction,
you will gradually be able to work up to
the darker tints, outside of each, so as quite
to efface their edges, and unite them tenderly
with the next tint. The whole square, when
done, should look evenly shaded from dark
to pale, with no bars, only a crossing texture
of touches, something like chopped straw, over
the whole.[1]

66. Next, take your rounded pebble; arrange it in any light and shade you like;
outline it very loosely with the pencil. Put
on a wash of colour, prepared *very* pale,
quite flat over all of it, except the highest
light, leaving the edge of your colour quite
sharp. Then another wash, extending only

---

[1] The use of acquiring this habit of execution is that
you may be able, when you begin to colour, to let one
hue be seen in minute portions, gleaming between the
touches of another.

over the darker parts, leaving the edge of that sharp also, as in tinting the square. Then another wash over the still darker parts, and another over the darkest, leaving each edge to dry sharp. Then, with the small touches, efface the edges, reinforce the darks, and work the whole delicately together as you would with the pen, till you have got it to the likeness of the true light and shade. You will find that the tint underneath is a great help, and that you can now get effects much more subtle and complete than with the pen merely.

67. The use of leaving the edges always sharp is that you may not trouble or vex the colour, but let it lie as it falls suddenly on the paper: colour looks much more lovely when it has been laid on with a dash of the brush, and left to dry in its own way, than when it has been dragged about and disturbed; so that it is always better to let the edges and forms be a little wrong, even if one cannot correct them afterwards, than to lose this fresh quality of the tint. Very great masters in water colour can lay on the true forms at once with a dash, and bad masters in water

colour lay on grossly false forms with a dash, and leave them false; for people in general, not knowing false from true, are as much pleased with the appearance of power in the irregular blot as with the presence of power in the determined one; but *we*, in our beginnings, must do as much as we can with the broad dash, and then correct with the point, till we are quite right. We must take care to be right, at whatever cost of pains; and then gradually we shall find we can be right with freedom.

68. I have hitherto limited you to colour mixed with two or three teaspoonfuls of water; but, in finishing your light and shade from the stone, you may, as you efface the edge of the palest coat towards the light, use the colour for the small touches with more and more water, till it is so pale as not to be perceptible. Thus you may obtain a perfect gradation to the light. And in reinforcing the darks, when they are very dark, you may use less and less water. If you take the colour tolerably dark on your brush, only always liquid (not pasty), and dash away the superfluous colour on blotting paper,

you will find that, touching the paper very
lightly with the dry brush, you can, by repeated touches, produce a dusty kind of
bloom, very valuable in giving depth to
shadow; but it requires great patience and
delicacy of hand to do this properly. You
will find much of this kind of work in the
grounds and shadows of William Hunt's
drawings.[1]

69. As you get used to the brush and
colour, you will gradually find out their ways
for yourself, and get the management of them.
And you will often save yourself much dis-
couragement by remembering what I have so
often asserted,—that if anything goes wrong,
it is nearly sure to be refinement that is
wanting, not force; and connexion, not alteration. If you dislike the state your drawing
is in, do not lose patience with it, nor dash
at it, nor alter its plan, nor rub it desperately
out, at the place you think wrong; but look
if there are no shadows you can gradate
more perfectly; no little gaps and rents you
can fill; no forms you can more delicately
define: and do not *rush* at any of the errors

[1] William Hunt, of the Old Water-colour Society.

or incompletions thus discerned, but efface or supply slowly, and you will soon find your drawing take another look. A very useful expedient in producing some effects, is to wet the paper, and then lay the colour on it, more or less wet, according to the effect you want. You will soon see how prettily it gradates itself as it dries; when dry, you can reinforce it with delicate stippling when you want it darker. Also, while the colour is still damp on the paper, by drying your brush thoroughly, and touching the colour with the brush so dried, you may take out soft lights with great tenderness and precision. Try all sorts of experiments of this kind, noticing how the colour behaves; but remembering always that your final results must be obtained, and can only be obtained, by pure work with the point, as much as in the pen drawing.

70. You will find also, as you deal with more and more complicated subjects, that Nature's resources in light and shade are so much richer than yours, that you cannot possibly get all, or anything like all, the gradations of shadow in any given group. When this is the case, determine first to keep the

broad masses of things distinct : if, for instance, there is a green book, and a white piece of paper, and a black inkstand in the group, be sure to keep the white paper as a light mass, the green book as a middle tint mass, the black inkstand as a dark mass; and do not shade the folds in the paper, or corners of the book, so as to equal in depth the darkness of the inkstand.   The great difference between the masters of light and shade, and imperfect artists, is the power of the former to draw so delicately as to express form in a dark-coloured object with little light, and in a light-coloured object with little darkness; and it is better even to leave the forms here and there unsatisfactorily rendered than to lose the general relations of the great masses. And this, observe, not because masses are grand or desirable things in your composition (for with composition at present you have nothing whatever to do), but because it is a fact that things do so present themselves to the eyes of men, and that we see paper, book, and inkstand as three separate things, before we see the wrinkles, or chinks, or corners of any of the three.   Understand, therefore, at

once, that no detail can be as strongly expressed in drawing as it is in reality; and
strive to keep all your shadows and marks
and minor markings on the masses, lighter
than they appear to be in Nature; you are
sure otherwise to get them too dark.   You
will in doing this find that you cannot get
the projection of things sufficiently shown;
but never mind that; there is no need that
they should appear to project, but great need
that their relations of shade to each other
should be preserved.   All deceptive projection
is obtained by partial exaggeration of shadow;
and whenever you see it, you may be sure
the drawing is more or less bad: a thoroughly
fine drawing or painting will always show a
slight tendency towards flatness.

71. Observe, on the other hand, that, however white an object may be, there is always
some small point of it whiter than the rest.
You must therefore have a slight tone of grey
over everything in your picture except on the
extreme high lights; even the piece of white
paper, in your subject, must be toned slightly
down, unless (and there are thousand chances
against its being so) it should all be turned

so as fully to front the light. By examining
the treatment of the white objects in any
pictures accessible to you by Paul Veronese
or Titian, you will soon understand this.[1]

72. As soon as you feel yourself capable of
expressing with the brush the undulations of
surfaces and the relations of masses, you may
proceed to draw more complicated and beautiful
things.[2] And first, the boughs of trees, now not
in mere dark relief, but in full rounding. Take
the first bit of branch or stump that comes to
hand, with a fork in it; cut off the ends of the

---

[1] At Marlborough House, [in 1857] among the four principal
examples of Turner's later water-colour drawing, perhaps
the most neglected was that of fishing-boats and fish at sunset.
It is one of his most wonderful works, though unfinished.
If you examine the larger white fishing-boat sail, you will
find it has a little spark of pure white in its right-hand upper
corner, about as large as a minute pin's head, and that all
the surface of the sail is gradated to that focus. Try to copy
this sail once or twice, and you will begin to understand
Turner's work. Similarly, the wing of the Cupid in Correggio's large picture in the National Gallery is focussed to
two little grains of white at the top of it. The points of
light on the white flower in the wreath round the head of
the dancing child-faun, in Titian's Bacchus and Ariadne,
exemplify the same thing.

[2] I shall not henceforward number the exercises recommended; as they are distinguished only by increasing difficulty
of subject, not by difference of method.

forking branches, so as to leave the whole only about a foot in length ; get a piece of paper the same size, fix your bit of branch in some place where its position will not be altered, and draw it thoroughly, in all its light and shade, full size; striving, above all things, to get an accurate expression of its structure at the fork of the branch.   When once you have mastered the tree at its *armpits*, you will have little more trouble with it.

73. Always draw whatever the background happens to be, exactly as you see it.   Wherever you have fastened the bough, you must draw whatever is behind it, ugly or not, else you will never know whether the light and shade are right ; they may appear quite wrong to you, only for want of the background.   And this general law is to be observed in all your studies : whatever you draw, draw completely and unalteringly, else you never know if what you have done is right, or whether you *could* have done it rightly had you tried.   There is nothing *visible* out of which you may not get useful practice.

74. Next, to put the leaves on your boughs. Gather a small twig with four or five leaves on

it, put it into water, put a sheet of light-coloured or white paper behind it, so that all the leaves may be relieved in dark from the white field;

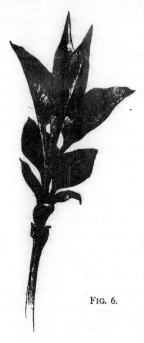

FIG. 6.

then sketch in their dark shape carefully with pencil as you did the complicated boughs, in order to be sure that all their masses and interstices are right in shape before you begin shading, and complete as far as you can with pen and ink, in the manner of Fig. 6, which is a young shoot of lilac.

75. You will probably, in spite of all your pattern drawings, be at first puzzled by leaf foreshortening; especially because the look of retirement or projection depends not so much on the perspective of the leaves themselves as on the double sight of the two eyes. Now there are certain artifices by which good painters can partly conquer this difficulty; as slight exaggerations of force or colour in the nearer parts, and of obscurity in the more distant ones; but you must not attempt anything of this kind. When you are first sketching the leaves, shut one of your eyes, fix a point in the background, to bring the point of one of the leaves against; and so sketch the whole bough as you see it in a fixed position, looking with one eye only. Your drawing never can be made to look like the object itself, as you see that object with *both* eyes,[1] but it can be made perfectly like

[1] If you understand the principle of the stereoscope you will know why ; if not, it does not matter ; trust me for the truth of the statement, as I cannot explain the principle without diagrams and much loss of time. See, however, Note 1, in Appendix I.

the object seen with one, and you must be content when you have got a resemblance on these terms.

76. In order to get clearly at the notion of the thing to be done, take a single long leaf, hold it with its point towards you, and as flat as you can, so as to see nothing of it but its thinness, as if you wanted to know how thin it was; outline it so. Then slope it down gradually towards you, and watch it as it lengthens out to its full length, held perpendicularly down before you. Draw it in three or four different positions between these extremes, with its ribs as they appear in each position, and you will soon find out how it must be.

77. Draw first only two or three of the leaves; then larger clusters; and practise, in this way, more and more complicated pieces of bough and leafage, till you find you can master the most difficult arrangements, not consisting of more than ten or twelve leaves. You will find as you do this, if you have an opportunity of visiting any gallery of pictures, that you take a much more lively interest than before in the work of the great masters; you

will see that very often their best backgrounds
are composed of little more than a few sprays
of leafage, carefully studied, brought against
the distant sky; and that another wreath or
two form the chief interest of their foregrounds. If you live in London you may
test your progress *accurately* by the degree
of admiration you feel for the leaves of vine
round the head of the Bacchus, in Titian's
Bacchus and Ariadne. All this, however, will
not enable you to draw a mass of foliage.
You will find, on looking at any rich piece of
vegetation, that it is only one or two of the
nearer clusters that you can by any possibility
draw in this complete manner. The mass is
too vast, and too intricate, to be thus dealt
with.

78. You must now therefore have recourse
to some confused mode of execution, capable
of expressing the confusion of Nature. And,
first, you must understand what the character
of that confusion is. If you look carefully at
the outer sprays of any tree at twenty or thirty
yards' distance, you will see them defined
against the sky in masses, which, at first,
look quite definite; but if you examine them,

you will see, mingled with the real shapes of
leaves, many indistinct lines, which are, some
of them, stalks of leaves, and some, leaves
seen with the edge turned towards you, and
coming into sight in a broken way; for, supposing the real leaf shape to be as at *a*,
Fig. 7, this, when removed some yards from the
eye, will appear dark against the sky, as at *b*;

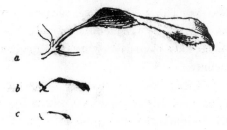

a

b

c

FIG. 7.

then, when removed some yards farther still,
the stalk and point disappear altogether, the
middle of the leaf becomes little more than
a line; and the result is the condition at *c*,
only with this farther subtlety in the look of
it, inexpressible in the woodcut, that the stalk
and point of the leaf, though they have dis-
appeared to the eye, have yet some influence
in *checking the light* at the places where they

F

exist, and cause a slight dimness about the
part of the leaf which remains visible, so that
its perfect effect could only be rendered by
two layers of colour, one subduing the sky
tone a little, the next drawing the broken
portions of the leaf, as at *c*, and carefully indicating the greater darkness of the spot in the
middle, where the under side of the leaf is.

This is the perfect theory of the matter.   In
practice we cannot reach such accuracy; but
we shall be able to render the general look of
the foliage satisfactorily by the following mode
of practice.

79. Gather a spray of any tree, about a foot
or eighteen inches long.   Fix it firmly by the
stem in anything that will support it steadily;
put it about eight feet away from you, or ten
if you are far-sighted.   Put a sheet of not very
white paper behind it, as usual.   Then draw
very carefully, first placing them with pencil,
and then filling them up with ink, every leaf-
mass and stalk of it in simple black profile, as
you see them against the paper: Fig. 8 is a
bough of Phillyrea so drawn.   Do not be afraid
of running the leaves into a black mass when
they come together; this exercise is only to

teach you what the actual shapes of such masses are when seen against the sky.

80. Make two careful studies of this kind of one bough of every common tree,—oak, ash, elm, birch, beech, &c.; in fact, if you

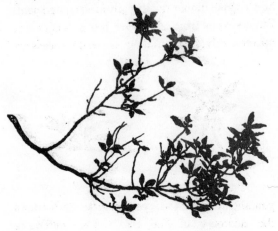

FIG. 8.

are good, and industrious, you will make one such study carefully at least three times a week, until you have examples of every sort of tree and shrub you can get branches of. You are to make two studies of each bough, for this reason,—all masses of foliage have

an upper and under surface, and the side
view of them, or profile, shows a wholly
different organisation of branches from that
seen in the view from above. They are
generally seen more or less in profile, as you
look at the whole tree, and Nature puts her
best composition into the profile arrangement.
But the view from above or below occurs not
unfrequently, also, and it is quite necessary

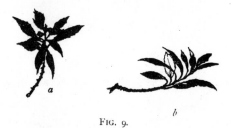

FIG. 9.

you should draw it if you wish to understand
the anatomy of the tree. The difference
between the two views is often far greater
than you could easily conceive. For instance,
in Fig. 9, *a* is the upper view and *b* the
profile, of a single spray of Phillyrea. Fig.
8 is an intermediate view of a larger bough ;
seen from beneath, but at some lateral distance
also.

81. When you have done a few branches in this manner, take one of the drawings you have made, and put it first a yard away from you, then a yard and a half, then two yards; observe how the thinner stalks and leaves gradually disappear, leaving only a vague and slight darkness where they were; and make another study of the effect at each distance, taking care to draw nothing more than you really see, for in this consists all the difference between what would be merely a miniature drawing of the leaves seen near, and a full-size drawing of the same leaves at a distance. By full size, I mean the size which they would really appear of if their outline were traced through a pane of glass held at the same distance from the eye at which you mean to hold your drawing. You can always ascertain this full size of any object by holding your paper upright before you, at the distance from your eye at which you wish your drawing to be seen. Bring its edge across the object you have to draw, and mark upon this edge the points where the outline of the object crosses, or goes behind, the edge of the paper. You will always

find it, thus measured, smaller than you supposed.

82. When you have made a few careful
experiments of this kind on your own drawings, (which are better for practice, at first,
than the real trees, because the black profile
in the drawing is quite stable, and does
not shake, and is not confused by sparkles
of lustre on the leaves,) you may try the
extremities of the real trees, only not doing
much at a time, for the brightness of the sky
will dazzle and perplex your sight. And
this brightness causes, I believe, some loss
of the outline itself; at least the chemical
action of the light in a photograph extends
much within the edges of the leaves, and, as
it were, eats them away, so that no tree extremity, stand it ever so still, nor any other
form coming against bright sky, is truly drawn
by a photograph; and if you once succeed
in drawing a few sprays rightly, you will find
the result much more lovely and interesting
than any photograph can be.

83. All this difficulty, however, attaches to
the rendering merely the dark form of the sprays
as they come against the sky. Within those

sprays, and in the heart of the tree, there is a
complexity of a much more embarrassing kind;
for nearly all leaves have some lustre, and
all are more or less translucent (letting light
through them); therefore, in any given leaf,
besides the intricacies of its own proper
shadows and foreshortenings, there are three
series of circumstances which alter or hide its
forms.   First, shadows cast on it by other
leaves,—often very forcibly.   Secondly, light
reflected from its lustrous surface, sometimes
the blue of the sky, sometimes the white of
clouds, or the sun itself flashing like a star.
Thirdly, forms and shadows of other leaves,
seen as darknesses through the translucent
parts of the leaf; a most important element
of foliage effect, but wholly neglected by
landscape artists in general.

84. The consequence of all this is, that
except now and then by chance, the form
of a complete leaf is never seen; but a marvellous and quaint confusion, very definite,
indeed, in its evidence of direction of growth,
and unity of action, but wholly indefinable
and inextricable, part by part, by any amount
of patience.   You cannot possibly work it

out in facsimile, though you took a twelve-
month's time to a tree; and you must therefore try to discover some mode of execution
which will more or less imitate, by its own
variety and mystery, the variety and mystery
of Nature, without absolute delineation of
detail.

85. Now I have led you to this conclusion
by observation of tree form only, because in
that the thing to be proved is clearest. But
no natural object exists which does not involve
in some part or parts of it this inimitable-
ness, this mystery of quantity, which needs
peculiarity of handling and trick of touch to
express it completely. If leaves are intricate,
so is moss, so is foam, so is rock cleavage, so
are fur and hair, and texture of drapery, and
of clouds. And although methods and dexterities of handling are wholly useless if you
have not gained first the thorough knowledge
of the form of the thing; so that if you cannot
draw a branch perfectly, then much less a
tree; and if not a wreath of mist perfectly,
much less a flock of clouds; and if not a
single grass blade perfectly, much less a grass
bank; yet having once got this power over

decisive form, you may safely—and must, in order to perfection of work—carry out your knowledge by every aid of method and dexterity of hand.

86. But, in order to find out what method can do, you must now look at Art as well as at Nature, and see what means painters and engravers have actually employed for the expression of these subtleties. Whereupon arises the question, what opportunity you have to obtain engravings? You ought, if it is at all in your power, to possess yourself of a certain number of good examples of Turner's engraved works: if this be not in your power, you must just make the best use you can of the shop windows, or of any plates of which you can obtain a loan. Very possibly, the difficulty of getting sight of them may stimulate you to put them to better use. But, supposing your means admit of your doing so, possess yourself, first, of the illustrated edition either of Rogers's Italy or Rogers's Poems, and then of about a dozen of the plates named in the annexed lists. The prefixed letters indicate the particular points deserving your study in each engrav-

ing.[1] Be sure, therefore, that your selection
includes, at all events, one plate marked with
each letter. Do not get more than twelve
of these plates, nor even all the twelve at
first ; for the more engravings you have, the

---

[1] The plates marked with a star are peculiarly desirable.
See note at the end of Appendix I. The letters mean as
follows :—

a stands for architecture, including distant grouping of towns,
    cottages, &c.
c clouds, including mist and aerial effects.
f foliage.
g ground, including low hills, when not rocky.
l effects of light.
m mountains, or bold rocky ground.
p power of general arrangement and effect.
q quiet water.
r running or rough water ; or rivers, even if calm, when their
    line of flow is beautifully marked.

From the England Series.

a c f r. Arundel.	*a f p.* Lancaster.
a f l. Ashby de la Zouche.	*c l m r.* Lancaster Sands.*
a l q r. Barnard Castle.*	*a g f.* Launceston.*
f m r. Bolton Abbey.	*c f l r.* Leicester Abbey.
f g r. Buckfastleigh.*	*f r.* Ludlow.
a l p. Caernarvon.	*a f l.* Margate.
c l q. Castle Upnor.	*a l q.* Orford.
a f l. Colchester.	*c p.* Plymouth.
l q. Cowes.	*f.* Powis Castle.
c f p. Dartmouth Cove.*	*l m q.* Prudhoe Castle.
c l q. Flint Castle.*	*f l m r.* Chain Bridge over
a f g l. Knaresborough.*	Tees.*

less attention you will pay to them. It is
a general truth, that the enjoyment derivable
from art cannot be increased in quantity,
beyond a certain point, by quantity of possession; it is only spread, as it were, over

m r. High Force of Tees.*	*m q*. Ulleswater.
a f q. Trematon.	*f m*. Valle Crucis.

From the Keepsake.

m p q. Arona.	*p*. St. Germain en Laye.
l m. Drachenfels.*	*l p q*. Florence.
f l. Marly.*	*l m*. Ballyburgh Ness.*

From the Bible Series.

f m. Mount Lebanon.	*a c g*. Joppa.
m. Rock of Moses at	*c l p q*. Solomon's Pools.*
Sinai.	*a l*. Santa Saba.
a l m. Jericho.	*a l*. Pool of Bethesda.

From Scott's Works.

p r. Melrose.*	*c m*. Glencoe.
f r. Dryburgh.*	*c m*. Loch Coriskin.*
	a l. Caerlaverock.

From the Rivers of France.

a q. Château of Amboise, with large bridge on right.	dral and rainbow, avenue on left.
	a p. Rouen Cathedral.
l p r. Rouen, looking down the river, poplars on right.*	*f p*. Pont de l'Arche.
	f l p. View on the Seine, with avenue.
a l p. Rouen, with cathe-	*a c p*. Bridge of Meulan.
	c g p r. Caudebec.*

a larger surface, and very often dulled by finding ideas repeated in different works. Now, for a beginner, it is always better that his attention should be concentrated on one or two good things, and all his enjoyment founded on them, than that he should look at many, with divided thoughts. He has much to discover; and his best way of discovering it is to think long over few things, and watch them earnestly. It is one of the worst errors of this age to try to know and to see too much: the men who seem to know everything, never in reality know anything rightly. Beware of *hand-book* knowledge.

87. These engravings are, in general, more for you to look at than to copy; and they will be of more use to you when we come to talk of composition, than they are at present; still, it will do you a great deal of good, sometimes to try how far you can get their delicate texture, or gradations of tone: as your pen-and-ink drawing will be apt to incline too much to a scratchy and broken kind of shade. For instance, the texture of the white convent wall, and the drawing of its tiled roof, in the vignette at p. 227 of

Rogers's Poems, is as exquisite as work can
possibly be; and it will be a great and profit-
able achievement if you can at all approach it.
In like manner, if you can at all imitate the
dark distant country at p. 7, or the sky at
p. 80, of the same volume, or the foliage at
pp. 12 and 144, it will be good gain; and
if you can once draw the rolling clouds and
running river at p. 9 of the Italy, or the city
in the vignette of Aosta at p. 25, or the
moonlight at p. 223, you will find that even
Nature herself cannot afterwards very terribly puzzle you with her torrents, or towers,
or moonlight.

88. You need not copy touch for touch,
but try to get the same effect. And if you
feel discouraged by the delicacy required, and
begin to think that engraving is not drawing, and that copying it cannot help you to
draw, remember that it differs from common
drawing only by the difficulties it has to
encounter. You perhaps have got into a
careless habit of thinking that engraving is
a mere business, easy enough when one has
got into the knack of it. On the contrary,
it is a form of drawing more difficult than

common drawing, by exactly so much as it is more difficult to cut steel than to move the pencil over paper. It is true that there are certain mechanical aids and methods which reduce it at certain stages either to pure machine work, or to more or less a habit of hand and arm; but this is not so in the foliage you are trying to copy, of which the best and prettiest parts are always etched— that is, drawn with a fine steel point and free hand: only the line made is white instead of black, which renders it much more difficult to judge of what you are about. And the trying to copy these plates will be good for you, because it will awaken you to the real labour and skill of the engraver, and make you understand a little how people must work, in this world, who have really to *do* anything in it.

89. Do not, however, suppose that I give you the engraving as a model—far from it; but it is necessary you should be able to do as well [1] before you think of doing better,

---

[1] As *well;*—not as minutely: the diamond cuts finer lines on the steel than you can draw on paper with your pen ; but you must be able to get tones as even, and touches as firm.

and you will find many little helps and hints
in the various work of it. Only remember
that *all* engravers' foregrounds are bad;
whenever you see the peculiar wriggling
parallel lines of modern engravings become
distinct, you must not copy; nor admire: it
is only the softer masses, and distances, and
portions of the foliage in the plates marked
f, which you may copy. The best for this
purpose, if you can get it, is the "Chain
bridge over the Tees," of the England series;
the thicket on the right is very beautiful
and instructive, and very like Turner. The
foliage in the "Ludlow" and "Powis" is also
remarkably good.

90. Besides these line engravings, and to
protect you from what harm there is in their
influence, you are to provide yourself, if
possible, with a Rembrandt etching, or a
photograph of one (of figures, not landscape).
It does not matter of what subject, or whether
a sketchy or finished one, but the sketchy
ones are generally cheapest, and will teach
you most. Copy it as well as you can,
noticing especially that Rembrandt's most
rapid lines have steady purpose; and that

they are laid with almost inconceivable precision when the object becomes at all interesting. The "Prodigal Son," "Death of
the Virgin," "Abraham and Isaac," and such
others, containing incident and character rather
than chiaroscuro, will be the most instructive.
You can buy one; copy it well; then ex-
change it, at little loss, for another; and so,
gradually, obtain a good knowledge of his
system. Whenever you have an opportunity
of examining his work at museums, &c., do
so with the greatest care, not looking at *many*
things, but a long time at each. You must
also provide yourself, if possible, with an
engraving of Albert Dürer's. This you will
not be able to copy; but you must keep it
beside you, and refer to it as a standard of
precision in line. If you can get one with a
wing in it, it will be best. The crest with the
cock, that with the skull and satyr, and the
"Melancholy," are the best you could have,
but any will do. Perfection in chiaroscuro
drawing lies between these two masters, Rembrandt and Dürer. Rembrandt is often too
loose and vague; and Dürer has little or
no effect of mist or uncertainty. If you can

see anywhere a drawing by Leonardo, you will find it balanced between the two characters; but there are no engravings which present this perfection, and your style will be best formed, therefore, by alternate study of Rembrandt and Dürer. Lean rather to Dürer; it is better, for amateurs, to err on the side of precision than on that of vagueness: and though, as I have just said, you cannot copy a Dürer, yet try every now and then a quarter of an inch square or so, and see how much nearer you can come; you cannot possibly try to draw the leafy crown of the "Melancholia" too often.

91. If you cannot get either a Rembrandt or a Dürer, you may still learn much by carefully studying any of George Cruikshank's etchings, or Leech's woodcuts in Punch, on the free side; with Alfred Rethel's and Richter's [1] on the severe side. But in so doing you will need to notice the following points:

92. When either the material (as the copper or wood) or the time of an artist does not

[1] See, for account of these plates, the Appendix on "Works to be studied."

G

permit him to make a perfect drawing,—that is to say, one in which no lines shall be prominently visible,—and he is reduced to show the black lines, either drawn by the pen, or on the wood, it is better to make these lines help, as far as may be, the expression of texture and form. You will thus find many textures, as of cloth or grass or flesh, and many subtle effects of light, expressed by Leech with zigzag or crossed or curiously broken lines; and you will see that Alfred Rethel and Richter constantly express the direction and rounding of surfaces by the direction of the lines which shade them. All these various means of expression will be useful to you, as far as you can learn them, provided you remember that they are merely a kind of shorthand; telling certain facts not in quite the right way, but in the only possible way under the conditions: and provided in any after use of such means, you never try to show your own dexterity; but only to get as much record of the object as you can in a given time; and that you continually make efforts to go beyond such shorthand, and draw portions of the objects rightly.

93. And touching this question of direction of lines as indicating that of surface, observe these few points:

If lines are to be distinctly shown, it is better that, so far as they *can* indicate anything by their direction, they should explain rather than oppose the general character of

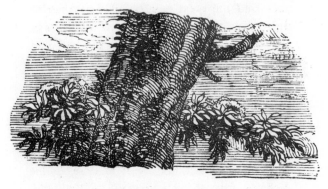

FIG. 10.

the object.   Thus, in the piece of woodcut from Titian, Fig. 10, the lines are serviceable by expressing, not only the shade of the trunk, but partly also its roundness, and the flow of its grain.   And Albert Dürer, whose work was chiefly engraving, sets himself always thus to make his lines as *valuable*

as possible; telling much by them, both of
shade and direction of surface: and if you
were always to be limited to engraving on
copper (and did not want to express effects of
mist or darkness, as well as delicate forms),
Albert Dürer's way of work would be the
best example for you.   But, inasmuch as the
perfect way of drawing is by shade without
lines, and the great painters always conceive
their subject as complete, even when they
are sketching it most rapidly, you will find
that, when they are not limited in means,
they do not much trust to direction of line,
but will often scratch in the shade of a
rounded surface with nearly straight lines,
that is to say, with the easiest and quickest
lines possible to themselves.   When the hand
is free, the easiest line for it to draw is one
inclining from the left upwards to the right,
or vice versâ, from the right downwards to the
left; and when done very quickly, the line
is hooked a little at the end by the effort
at return to the next.   Hence, you will always
find the pencil, chalk, or pen sketch of a
very great master full of these kind of lines;
and even if he draws carefully, you will find

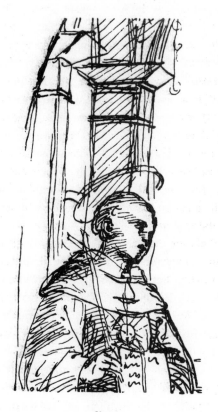

FIG. 11.

him using simple straight lines from left to
right, when an inferior master would have
used curved ones.   Fig. 11 is a fair facsimile
of part of a sketch of Raphael's, which exhibits these characters very distinctly.   Even
the careful drawings of Leonardo da Vinci are
shaded most commonly with straight lines; and
you may always assume it as a point increasing
the probability of a drawing being by a great
master if you find rounded surfaces, such as those
of cheeks or lips, shaded with straight lines.

94. But you will also now understand how
easy it must be for dishonest dealers to forge
or imitate scrawled sketches like Fig. 11, and
pass them for the work of great masters; and
how the power of determining the genuineness
of a drawing depends entirely on your knowing
the facts of the objects drawn, and perceiving
whether the hasty handling is *all* conducive to
the expression of those truths.   In a great
man's work, at its fastest, no line is thrown
away, and it is not by the rapidity, but the
economy of the execution that you know him
to be great.   Now to judge of this economy,
you must know exactly what he meant to
do, otherwise you cannot of course discern

how far he has done it; that is, you must
know the beauty and nature of the thing he
was drawing.   All judgment of art thus finally
founds itself on knowledge of Nature.

95. But farther observe, that this scrawled,
or economic, or impetuous execution is never
affectedly impetuous.   If a great man is not
in a hurry, he never pretends to be; if he
has no eagerness in his heart, he puts none
into his hand; if he thinks his effect would
be better got with *two* lines, he never, to show
his dexterity, tries to do it with one.   Be
assured, therefore (and this is a matter of
great importance), that you will never produce
a great drawing by imitating the execution of
a great master.   Acquire his knowledge and
share his feelings, and the easy execution
will fall from your hand as it did from his:
but if you merely scrawl because he scrawled,
or blot because he blotted, you will not only
never advance in power, but every able
draughtsman, and every judge whose opinion
is worth having, will know you for a cheat,
and despise you accordingly.

96. Again, observe respecting the use of
outline :

All merely outlined drawings are bad, for the simple reason, that an artist of any power can always do more, and tell more, by quitting his outlines occasionally, and scratching in a few lines for shade, than he can by restricting himself to outline only. Hence the fact of his so restricting himself, whatever may be the occasion, shows him to be a bad draughtsman, and not to know how to apply his power economically. This hard law, however, bears only on drawings meant to remain in the state in which you see them; not on those which were meant to be proceeded with, or for some mechanical use. It is sometimes necessary to draw pure outlines, as an incipient arrangement of a composition, to be filled up afterwards with colour, or to be pricked through and used as patterns or tracings; but if, with no such ultimate object, making the drawing wholly for its own sake, and meaning it to remain in the state he leaves it, an artist restricts himself to outline, he is a bad draughtsman, and his work is bad. There is no exception to this law. A good artist habitually sees masses, not edges, and can in every case make his drawing more expressive (with any given quantity of work) by rapid shade than by contours; so that all good work whatever is more or less touched with shade, and more or less interrupted as outline.

97. Hence, the published works of Retzsch, and all the English imitations of them, and all outline engravings from pictures, are bad work, and only serve to corrupt the public taste. And of such outlines, the worst are those which are darkened in some part of their course by way of expressing the dark side, as Flaxman's from Dante, and such others; because an outline can only be true so long as it accurately represents the form of the given object with *one* of its edges. Thus, the outline *a* and the outline *b*, Fig. 12, are both *true* outlines of a ball; because, however thick the line may be, whether we take the interior or exterior edge of it, that edge of it always draws a true circle. But *c* is a false outline of a ball, because either the inner or outer edge of the black line must be an untrue circle, else the line could not be thicker in one place than another. Hence all "force," as it is called, is gained by falsification

of the contours; so that no artist whose eye is true and fine could endure to look at it. It does indeed often happen that a painter, sketching rapidly, and trying again and again for some line which he cannot quite strike, blackens or loads the first line by setting others beside and across it; and then a careless observer supposes it has been thickened on purpose: or, sometimes also, at a place where shade is afterwards to enclose the form, the painter will strike a broad dash of this shade beside his outline at once, looking as if he meant to thicken the outline; whereas this broad line is only the first instalment of the future shadow, and the outline is really drawn with its inner edge.[1]   And thus, far from good draughtsmen darkening the lines which turn away from the light, the *tendency* with them is rather to darken them towards the light, for it is there in general that shade will ultimately enclose them.   The best example of this treatment that I know is Raphael's sketch, in the Louvre, of the head of the angel pursuing Heliodorus, the one that shows part of the left eye; where the

[1] See Note 2 in Appendix I.

dark strong lines which terminate the nose
and forehead towards the light are opposed
to tender and light ones behind the ear, and
in other places towards the shade. You will
see in Fig. 11 the same principle variously
exemplified; the principal dark lines, in the
head and drapery of the arms, being on the
side turned to the light.

98. All these refinements and ultimate principles, however, do not affect your drawing
for the present. You must try to make your
outlines as *equal* as possible; and employ pure
outline only for the two following purposes:
either (1.) to steady your hand, as in Exercise
II., for if you cannot draw the line itself, you
will never be able to terminate your shadow
in the precise shape required, when the line
is absent; or (2.) to give you shorthand
memoranda of forms, when you are pressed
for time. Thus the forms of distant trees
in groups are defined, for the most part, by
the light edge of the rounded mass of the
nearer one being shown against the darker
part of the rounded mass of a more distant
one; and to draw this properly, nearly as
much work is required to round each tree

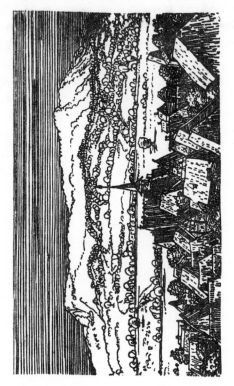

Fig. 13.

as to round the stone in Fig. 5.   Of course
you cannot often get time to do this; but if
you mark the terminal line of each tree as
is done by Dürer in Fig. 13, you will get a
most useful memorandum of their arrangement, and a very interesting drawing.   Only
observe in doing this, you must not, because
the procedure is a quick one, hurry that
procedure itself.   You will find, on copying
that bit of Dürer, that every one of his lines
is firm, deliberate, and accurately descriptive
as far as it goes.   It means a bush of such a
size and such a shape, definitely observed and
set down; it contains a true "signalement"
of every nut-tree, and apple-tree, and higher
bit of hedge, all round that village.   If you
have not time to draw thus carefully, do not
draw at all—you are merely wasting your
work and spoiling your taste.   When you
have had four or five years' practice you may
be able to make useful memoranda at a rapid
rate, but not yet; except sometimes of light
and shade, in a way of which I will tell you
presently.   And this use of outline, note
farther, is wholly confined to objects which
have edges or limits.   You can outline a tree

or a stone, when it rises against another tree
or stone; but you cannot outline folds in
drapery, or waves in water; if these are to
be expressed at all, it must be by some sort
of shade, and therefore the rule that no good
drawing can consist throughout of pure outline remains absolute.   You see, in that woodcut of Dürer's, his reason for even limiting
himself so much to outline as he has, in those
distant woods and plains, is that he may leave
them in bright light, to be thrown out still more
by the dark sky and the dark village spire: and
the scene becomes real and sunny only by the
addition of these shades.

99. Understanding, then, thus much of the
use of outline, we will go back to our question
about tree-drawing left unanswered at page 88.

We were, you remember, in pursuit of
mystery among the leaves. Now, it is quite
easy to obtain mystery and disorder, to any
extent; but the difficulty is to keep organiza-
tion in the midst of mystery. And you will
never succeed in doing this unless you lean
always to the definite side, and allow yourself rarely to become quite vague, at least
through all your early practice. So, after

your single groups of leaves, your first step
must be to conditions like Figs. 14 and 15,
which are careful facsimiles of two portions
of a beautiful woodcut of Dürer's, the "Flight
into Egypt." Copy these carefully, — never
mind how little at a time, but thoroughly ;

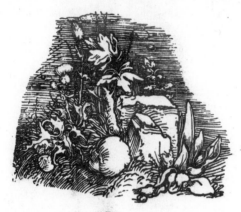

FIG. 14.

then trace the Dürer, and apply it to your
drawing, and do not be content till the one
fits the other, else your eye is not true enough
to carry you safely through meshes of real
leaves. And in the course of doing this, you
will find that not a line nor dot of Dürer's
can be displaced without harm ; that all add

to the effect, and either express something,
or illumine something, or relieve something.
If, afterwards, you copy any of the pieces
of modern tree drawing, of which so many
rich examples are given constantly in our

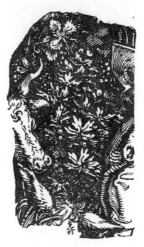

FIG. 15.

cheap illustrated periodicals (any of the Christmas numbers of last year's *Illustrated News*
or others are full of them), you will see that,
though good and forcible general effect is produced, the lines are thrown in by thousands

without special intention, and might just as
well go one way as another, so only that
there be enough of them to produce all together a well-shaped effect of intricacy: and
you will find that a little careless scratching about with your pen will bring you very
near the same result without an effort; but
that no scratching of pen, nor any fortunate
chance, nor anything but downright skill and
thought, will imitate so much as one leaf of
Dürer's. Yet there is considerable intricacy
and glittering confusion in the interstices of
those vine leaves of his, as well as of the
grass. .

100. When you have got familiarised to his
firm manner, you may draw from Nature as
much as you like in the same way; and when
you are tired of the intense care required for
this, you may fall into a little more easy
massing of the leaves, as in Fig. 10 (p. 99).
This is facsimiléd from an engraving after
Titian, but an engraving not quite first-rate
in manner, the leaves being a little too formal;
still, it is a good enough model for your times
of rest; and when you cannot carry the thing
even so far as this, you may sketch the forms

H

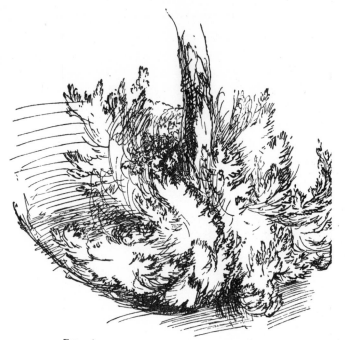

FIG. 16.

of the masses, as in Fig. 16,[1] taking care
always to have thorough command over your
hand; that is, not to let the mass take a free
shape because your hand ran glibly over the
paper, but because in Nature it has actually
a free and noble shape, and you have faithfully
followed the same.

101. And now that we have come to questions of noble shape, as well as true shape, and
that we are going to draw from Nature at our
pleasure, other considerations enter into the
business, which are by no means confined to
first practice, but extend to all practice; these
(as this letter is long enough, I should think,
to satisfy even the most exacting of corre-
spondents) I will arrange in a second letter;
praying you only to excuse the tiresomeness
of this first one — tiresomeness inseparable
from directions touching the beginning of any
art,—and to believe me, even though I am
trying to set you to dull and hard work,

Very faithfully yours,

J. RUSKIN.

---

[1] This sketch is not of a tree standing on its head, though
it looks like it. You will find it explained presently.

LETTER II.

SKETCHING FROM NATURE.

102. MY DEAR READER,—The work we have already gone through together has, I hope, enabled you to draw with fair success either rounded and simple masses, like stones, or complicated arrangements of form, like those of leaves; provided only these masses or complexities will stay quiet for you to copy, and do not extend into quantity so great as to baffle your patience. But if we are now to go out to the fields, and to draw anything like a complete landscape, neither of these conditions will any more be observed for us. The clouds will not wait while we copy their heaps or clefts; the shadows will escape from us as we try to shape them, each, in its stealthy minute march, still leaving light where its tremulous edge had rested the moment before, and involving in eclipse objects that had

seemed safe from its influence; and instead
of the small clusters of leaves which we could
reckon point by point, embarrassing enough
even though numerable, we have now leaves
as little to be counted as the sands of the sea,
and restless, perhaps, as its foam.

103. In all that we have to do now, therefore, direct imitation becomes more or less
impossible. It is always to be aimed at so
far as it *is* possible; and when you have
time and opportunity, some portions of a
landscape may, as you gain greater skill, be
rendered with an approximation almost to
mirrored portraiture. Still, whatever skill
you may reach, there will always be need
of judgment to choose, and of speed to seize,
certain things that are principal or fugitive;
and you must give more and more effort daily
to the observance of characteristic points, and
the attainment of concise methods.

104. I have directed your attention early
to foliage for two reasons. First, that it is
always accessible as a study; and secondly,
that its modes of growth present simple
examples of the importance of leading or
governing lines. It is by seizing these leading

lines, when we cannot seize all, that likeness and expression are given to a portrait,
and grace and a kind of vital truth to the
rendering of every natural form. I call it
vital truth, because these chief lines are
always expressive of the past history and
present action of the thing. They show in a
mountain, first, how it was built or heaped
up; and secondly, how it is now being worn
away, and from what quarter the wildest
storms strike it. In a tree, they show what
kind of fortune it has had to endure from
its childhood: how troublesome trees have
come in its way, and pushed it aside, and
tried to strangle or starve it; where and when
kind trees have sheltered it, and grown up
lovingly together with it, bending as it bent;
what winds torment it most; what boughs
of it behave best, and bear most fruit; and
so on. In a wave or cloud, these leading
lines show the run of the tide and of the
wind, and the sort of change which the water
or vapour is at any moment enduring in its
form, as it meets shore, or counter-wave, or
melting sunshine. Now remember, nothing
distinguishes great men from inferior men

more than their always, whether in life or
in art, *knowing the way things are going.*
Your dunce thinks they are standing still,
and draws them all fixed ; your wise man
sees the change or changing in them, and
draws them so,—the animal in its motion,
the tree in its growth, the cloud in its
course, the mountain in its wearing away.
Try always, whenever you look at a form,
to see the lines in it which have had power
over its past fate and will have power over
its futurity. Those are its *awful* lines ; see
that you seize on those, whatever else you
miss. Thus, the leafage in Fig. 16 (p. 114)
grew round the root of a stone pine, on the
brow of a crag at Sestri near Genoa, and all
the sprays of it are thrust away in their first
budding by the great rude root, and spring
out in every direction round it, as water
splashes when a heavy stone is thrown into
it. Then, when they have got clear of the
root, they begin to bend up again ; some of
them, being little stone pines themselves, have
a great notion of growing upright, if they
can ; and this struggle of theirs to recover
their straight road towards the sky, after

being obliged to grow sideways in their early
years, is the effort that will mainly influence
their future destiny, and determine if they
are to be crabbed, forky pines, striking from
that rock of Sestri, whose clefts nourish
them, with bared red lightning of angry arms
towards the sea; or if they are to be goodly
and solemn pines, with trunks like pillars of
temples, and the purple burning of their
branches sheathed in deep globes of cloudy
green. Those, then, are their fateful lines;
see that you give that spring and resilience,
whatever you leave ungiven: depend upon it,
their chief beauty is in these.

105. So in trees in general, and bushes,
large or small, you will notice that, though
the boughs spring irregularly and at various
angles, there is a tendency in all to stoop
less and less as they near the top of the
tree. This structure, typified in the simplest
possible terms at *c*, Fig. 17, is common to
all trees that I know of, and it gives them a
certain plumy character, and aspect of unity
in the hearts of their branches which are
essential to their beauty. The stem does
not merely send off a wild branch here and

there to take its own way, but all the branches
share in one great fountain-like impulse; each
has a curve and a path to take, which fills
a definite place, and each terminates all its
minor branches at its outer extremity, so as
to form a great outer curve, whose character
and proportion are peculiar for each species.
That is to say, the general type or idea of
a tree is not as *a*, Fig. 17, but as *b*, in

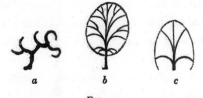

a   *b*   *c*

FIG. 17.

which, observe, the boughs all carry their
minor divisions right out to the bounding
curve; not but that smaller branches, by
thousands, terminate in the heart of the tree,
but the idea and main purpose in every
branch are to carry all its child branches
well out to the air and light, and let each of
them, however small, take its part in filling
the united flow of the bounding curve, so

that the type of each separate bough is again
not *a*, but *b*, Fig. 18; approximating, that is
to say, so far to the structure of a plant of

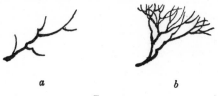

a   *b*

FIG. 18.

broccoli as to throw the great mass of spray
and leafage out to a rounded surface.   Therefore beware of getting into a careless habit
of drawing boughs with successive sweeps of
the pen or brush, one hanging to the other,
as in Fig. 19.   If you look at the tree-boughs

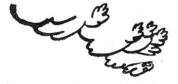

FIG. 19.

in any painting of Wilson's you will see
this structure, and nearly every other that is
to be avoided, in their intensest types.   You
will also notice that Wilson never conceives

a tree as a round mass, but flat, as if it had been pressed and dried. Most people in drawing pines seem to fancy, in the same way, that the boughs come out only on two sides of the trunk, instead of all round it: always, therefore, take more pains in trying to draw the boughs of trees that grow *towards* you than those that go off to the sides; anybody can draw the latter, but the foreshortened ones are not so easy. It will help you in drawing them to observe that in most trees the ramification of each branch, though not of the tree itself, is more or less flattened, and approximates, in its position, to the look of a hand held out to receive something, or shelter something. If you take a looking-glass, and hold your hand before it slightly hollowed, with the palm upwards, and the fingers open, as if you were going to support the base of some great bowl, larger than you could easily hold; and sketch your hand as you see it in the glass with the points of the fingers towards you; it will materially help you in understanding the way trees generally hold out their hands: and if then you will turn yours with its palm downwards, as if you were going to try to hide something, but with the fingers expanded, you will get a good type of the action of the lower boughs in cedars and such other spreading trees.

106. Fig. 20 will give you a good idea of the simplest way in which these and other such facts can be rapidly expressed; if you copy it carefully, you will be surprised to find how the touches all group together, in expressing the plumy toss of the tree branches, and the springing of the bushes out of the bank, and the undulation of the ground: note the careful drawing of the footsteps made by the climbers of the little mound on the left.[1] It is facsimiled from an etching of Turner's, and is as good an example as you can have of the use of pure and firm lines; it will also show you how the particular action in foliage, or anything else to which you wish to direct attention, may be intensified by the adjuncts. The tall and upright trees are made to look more tall and upright still, because their line is continued below by the figure of the farmer with his stick; and the

[1] It is meant, I believe, for " Salt Hill."

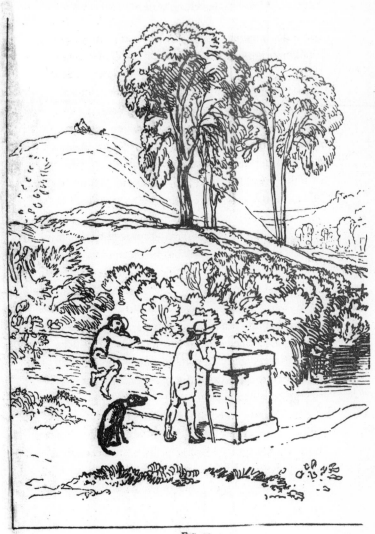

FIG. 20.

rounded bushes on the bank are made to look more rounded because their line is continued in one broad sweep by the black dog and the boy climbing the wall. These figures are placed entirely with this object, as we shall see more fully hereafter when we come to talk about composition; but, if you please, we will not talk about that yet awhile. What I have been telling you about the beautiful lines and action of foliage has nothing to do with composition, but only with fact, and the brief and expressive representation of fact. But there will be no harm in your looking forward, if you like to do so, to the account, in Letter III. of the "Law of Radiation," and reading what is said there about tree growth: indeed it would in some respects have been better to have said it here than there, only it would have broken up the account of the principles of composition somewhat awkwardly.

107. Now, although the lines indicative of action are not always quite so manifest in other things as in trees, a little attention will soon enable you to see that there are such lines in everything. In an old house roof,

a bad observer and bad draughtsman will
only see and draw the spotty irregularity of
tiles or slates all over; but a good draughtsman will see all the bends of the under
timbers, where they are weakest and the
weight is telling on them most, and the tracks
of the run of the water in time of rain, where
it runs off fastest, and where it lies long
and feeds the moss; and he will be careful,
however few slates he draws, to mark the
way they bend together towards those hollows
(which have the future fate of the roof in
them), and crowd gradually together at the top
of the gable, partly diminishing in perspective,
partly, perhaps, diminished on purpose (they
are so in most English old houses) by the
slate-layer. So in ground, there is always
the direction of the run of the water to be
noticed, which rounds the earth and cuts it
into hollows; and, generally, in any bank or
height worth drawing, a trace of bedded or
other internal structure besides. Figure 20
will give you some idea of the way in which
such facts may be expressed by a few lines.
Do you not feel the depression in the ground
all down the hill where the footsteps are, and

how the people always turn to the left at the top, losing breath a little, and then how the water runs down in that other hollow towards the valley, behind the roots of the trees ?

108. Now, I want you in your first sketches from Nature to aim exclusively at understanding and representing these vital facts of form ; using the pen—not now the steel, but the quill—firmly and steadily, never scrawling with it, but saying to yourself before you lay on a single touch,—" *that* leaf is the main one, *that* bough is the guiding one, and this touch, *so* long, *so* broad, means that part of it,"—point or side or knot, as the case may be. Resolve always, as you look at the thing, what you will take, and what miss of it, and never let your hand run away with you, or get into any habit or method of touch. If you want a continuous line, your hand should pass calmly from one end of it to the other without a tremor; if you want a shaking and broken line, your hand should shake, or break off, as easily as a musician's finger shakes or stops on a note: only remember this, that there is no general way of doing *any* thing; no recipe

can be given you for so much as the drawing
of a cluster of grass.   The grass may be
ragged and stiff, or tender and flowing; sun-
burnt and sheep-bitten, or rank and languid;
fresh or dry; lustrous or dull: look at it,
and try to draw it as it is, and don't think
how somebody "told you to *do* grass."   So
a stone may be round or angular, polished
or rough, cracked all over like an ill-glazed
teacup, or as united and broad as the breast
of Hercules.   It may be as flaky as a wafer,
as powdery as a field puff-ball; it may be
knotted like a ship's hawser, or kneaded like
hammered iron, or knit like a Damascus sabre,
or fused like a glass bottle, or crystallised like
hoar-frost, or veined like a forest leaf: look at
it, and don't try to remember how anybody
told you to "do a stone."

109. As soon as you find that your hand
obeys you thoroughly, and that you can
render any form with a firmness and truth
approaching that of Turner's or Dürer's work,[1]

---

[1] I do not mean that you can approach Turner or
Dürer in their strength, that is to say, in their imagination or power of design.   But you may approach them, by
perseverance, in truth of manner.

I

you must add a simple but equally careful
light and shade to your pen drawing, so as
to make each study as complete as possible ;
for which you must prepare yourself thus.
Get, if you have the means, a good impression of one plate of Turner's Liber Studiorum ;
if possible, one of the subjects named in the
note below.[2] If you cannot obtain, or even

[2] The following are the most desirable plates : —

Grande Chartreuse.
Æsacus and Hesperie.
Cephalus and Procris.
Source of Arveron.
Ben Arthur.
Watermill.
Hindhead Hill.
Hedging and Ditching.
Dumblane Abbey.
Morpeth.
Calais Pier.
Pembury Mill.

Little Devil's Bridge.
River Wye (*not* Wye and Se-
vern).
Holy Island.
Clyde.
Lauffenburg.
Blair Athol.
Alps from Grenoble.
Raglan. (Subject with quiet
brook, trees, and castle
on the right.)

If you cannot get one of these, any of the others will be
serviceable, except only the twelve following, which are
quite useless : —

1. Scene in Italy, with goats on a walled road, and trees
above.
2. Interior of church.
3. Scene with bridge, and trees above ; figures on left, one
playing a pipe.
4. Scene with figure playing on tambourine.

borrow for a little while, any of these engravings, you must use a photograph instead
(how, I will tell you presently); but, if you
can get the Turner, it will be best. You will
see that it is composed of a firm etching in
line, with mezzotint shadow laid over it. You
must first copy the etched part of it accurately ;
to which end put the print against the window,
and trace slowly with the greatest care every
black line; retrace this on smooth drawing-

   5. Scene on Thames with high trees, and a square tower
      of a church seen through them.
   6. Fifth Plague of Egypt.
   7. Tenth Plague of Egypt.
   8. Rivaulx Abbey.
   9. Wye and Severn.
  10. Scene with castle in centre, cows under trees on the
      left.
  11. Martello Towers.
  12. Calm.

It is very unlikely that you should meet with one of the
original etchings ; if you should, it will be a drawing-master
in itself alone, for it is not only equivalent to a pen-and-
ink drawing by Turner, but to a very careful one ; only
observe, the Source of Arveron, Raglan, and Dumblane were
not etched by Turner ; and the etchings of those three are
not good for separate study, though it is deeply interesting
to see how Turner, apparently provoked at the failure of
the beginnings in the Arveron and Raglan, took the plates
up himself, and either conquered or brought into use the bad
etching by his marvellous engraving. The Dumblane was,

paper; and, finally, go over the whole with
your pen, looking at the original plate always,
so that if you err at all, it may be on the
right side, not making a line which is too
curved or too straight already in the tracing,
more curved or more straight, as you go over
it.   And in doing this, never work after you
are tired, nor to "get the thing done," for if
it is badly done, it will be of no use to you.
The true zeal and patience of a quarter of
an hour are better than the sulky and in-
attentive labour of a whole day.   If you have
not made the touches right at the first going

however, well etched by Mr. Lupton, and beautifully engraved by him.   The finest Turner etching is of an aqueduct
with a stork standing in a mountain stream, not in the
published series ; and next to it, are the unpublished etchings
of the Via Mala and Crowhurst.   Turner seems to have been
so fond of these plates that he kept retouching and finishing
them, and never made up his mind to let them go.   The
Via Mala is certainly, in the state in which Turner left it,
the finest of the whole series : its etching is, as I said, the
best after that of the aqueduct.   Figure 20, above, is part
of another fine unpublished etching, "Windsor, from Salt
Hill."   Of the published etchings, the finest are the Ben
Arthur, Æsacus, Cephalus, and Stone Pines, with the Girl
washing at a Cistern ; the three latter are the more generally
instructive.   Hindhead Hill, Isis, Jason, and Morpeth, are
also very desirable.

over with the pen, retouch them delicately, with little ink in your pen, thickening or reinforcing them as they need : you cannot give too much care to the facsimile. Then keep this etched outline by you in order to study at your ease the way in which Turner uses his line as preparatory for the subsequent shadow ;[3] it is only in getting the two separate that you will be able to reason on this. Next, copy once more, though for the fourth time, any part of this etching which you like, and put on the light and shade with the brush, and any brown colour that matches that of the plate ;[4] working it with the point of the brush as delicately as if you were drawing with pencil, and dotting and cross-hatching as lightly as you can touch the paper, till you get the gradations of Turner's engraving.

110. In this exercise, as in the former one, a quarter of an inch worked to close resemblance of the copy is worth more than the whole subject carelessly done. Not that in

[3] You will find more notice of this point in the account of Harding's tree-drawing, a little farther on.

[4] The impressions vary so much in colour that no brown can be specified.

drawing afterwards from Nature you are to
be obliged to finish every gradation in this
way, but that, once having fully accomplished
the drawing *something* rightly, you will thenceforward feel and aim at a higher perfection
than you could otherwise have conceived, and
the brush will obey you, and bring out quickly
and clearly the loveliest results, with a sub-
missiveness which it would have wholly refused
if you had not put it to severest work. Nothing is more strange in art than the way
that chance and materials seem to favour you,
when once you have thoroughly conquered
them. Make yourself quite independent of
chance, get your result in spite of it, and
from that day forward all things will somehow
fall as you would have them. Show the
camel's hair, and the colour in it, that no
bending nor blotting is of any use to escape
your will; that the touch and the shade *shall*
finally be right, if it costs you a year's toil;
and from that hour of corrective conviction,
said camel's hair will bend itself to all your
wishes, and no blot will dare to transgress
its appointed border. If you cannot obtain
a print from the Liber Studiorum, get a

photograph [1] of some general landscape subject, with high hills and a village or picturesque town, in the middle distance, and some calm water of varied character (a stream with stones in it, if possible), and copy any part of it you like, in this same brown colour, working, as I have just directed you to do from the Liber, a great deal with the point of the brush. You are under a twofold disadvantage here, however; first, there are portions in every photograph too delicately done for you at present to be at all able to copy; and, secondly, there are portions always more obscure or dark than there would be in the real scene, and involved in a mystery which you will not be able, as yet, to decipher. Both these characters will be advantageous to you for future study, after you have gained experience, but they are a little against you in early attempts at tinting; still you must fight through the difficulty, and get the power of producing delicate gradations with brown or grey, like those of the photograph.

111. Now observe; the perfection of work

[1] You had better get such a photograph, even though you have a Liber print as well.

would be tinted shadow, like photography, without any obscurity or exaggerated darkness; and as long as your effect depends in anywise on visible lines, your art is not perfect, though it may be first-rate of its kind. But to get complete results in tints merely, requires both long time and consummate skill; and you will find that a few well-put pen lines, with a tint dashed over or under them, get more expression of facts than you could reach in any other way, by the same expenditure of time. The use of the Liber Studiorum print to you is chiefly as an example of the simplest shorthand of this kind, a shorthand which is yet capable of dealing with the most subtle natural effects; for the firm etching gets at the expression of complicated details, as leaves, masonry, textures of ground, &c., while the overlaid tint enables you to express the most tender distances of sky, and forms of playing light, mist, or cloud. Most of the best drawings by the old masters are executed on this principle, the touches of the pen being useful also to give a look of transparency to shadows, which could not otherwise be attained but by great finish of tinting; and if you have access

to any ordinarily good public gallery, or can
make friends of any printsellers who have
folios either of old drawings, or facsimiles of
them, you will not be at a loss to find some
example of this unity of pen with tinting.
Multitudes of photographs also are now taken
from the best drawings by the old masters,
and I hope that our Mechanics' Institutes and
other societies organised with a view to public
instruction, will not fail to possess themselves
of examples of these, and to make them accessible to students of drawing in the vicinity;
a single print from Turner's Liber, to show
the unison of tint with pen etching, and the
"St. Catherine," photographed by Thurston
Thompson from Raphael's drawing in the
Louvre, to show the unity of the soft tinting
of the stump with chalk, would be all that is
necessary, and would, I believe, be in many
cases more serviceable than a larger collection,
and certainly than a whole gallery of second-
rate prints.   Two such examples are peculiarly
desirable, because all other modes of drawing,
with pen separately, or chalk separately, or
colour separately, may be seen by the poorest
student in any cheap illustrated book, or in

shop windows.   But this unity of tinting with
line he cannot generally see but by some
special enquiry, and in some out of the way
places he could not find a single example of
it.   Supposing that this should be so in your
own case, and that you cannot meet with any
example of this kind, try to make the matter
out alone, thus :

112. Take a small and simple photograph ;
allow yourself half an hour to express its
subjects with the pen only, using some permanent liquid colour instead of ink, out-
lining its buildings or trees firmly, and laying
in the deeper shadows, as you have been
accustomed to do in your bolder pen drawings ;
then, when this etching is dry, take your
sepia or grey, and tint it over, getting now
the finer gradations of the photograph ; and,
finally taking out the higher lights with penknife or blotting paper.   You will soon find
what can be done in this way ; and by a
series of experiments you may ascertain for
yourself how far the pen may be made
serviceable to reinforce shadows, mark characters of texture, outline unintelligible masses,
and so on.   The more time you have, the

more delicate you may make the pen drawing,
blending it with the tint; the less you have,
the more distinct you must keep the two.
Practise in this way from one photograph,
allowing yourself sometimes only a quarter
of an hour for the whole thing, sometimes an
hour, sometimes two or three hours; in each
case drawing the whole subject in full depth
of light and shade, but with such degree of
finish in the parts as is possible in the given
time.   And this exercise, observe, you will do
well to repeat frequently, whether you can get
prints and drawings as well as photographs,
or not.

113. And now at last, when you can copy
a piece of Liber Studiorum, or its photographic
substitute, faithfully, you have the complete
means in your power of working from Nature
on all subjects that interest you, which you
should do in four different ways.

First. When you have full time, and your
subject is one that will stay quiet for you,
make perfect light and shade studies, or as
nearly perfect as you can, with grey or brown
colour of any kind, reinforced and defined
with the pen.

114. Secondly. When your time is short, or the subject is so rich in detail that you feel you cannot complete it intelligibly in light and shade, make a hasty study of the effect, and give the rest of the time to a Düreresque expression of the details. If the subject seems to you interesting, and there are points about it which you cannot understand, try to get five spare minutes to go close up to it, and make a nearer memorandum; not that you are ever to bring the details of this nearer sketch into the farther one, but that you may thus perfect your experience of the aspect of things, and know that such and such a look of a tower or cottage at five hundred yards off means *that* sort of tower or cottage near; while, also, this nearer sketch will be useful to prevent any future misinterpretation of your own work. If you have time, however far your light and shade study in the distance may have been carried, it is always well, for these reasons, to make also your Düreresque and your near memoranda; for if your light and shade drawing be good, much of the interesting detail must be lost in it, or disguised.

115. Your hasty study of effect may be made most easily and quickly with a soft pencil, dashed over when done with one tolerably deep tone of grey, which will fix the pencil. While this fixing colour is wet, take out the higher lights with the dry brush; and, when it is quite dry, scratch out the highest lights with the penknife. Five minutes, carefully applied, will do much by these means. Of course the paper is to be white. I do not like studies on grey paper so well; for you can get more gradation by the taking off your wet tint, and laying it on cunningly a little.darker here and there, than you can with body-colour white, unless you are consummately skilful. There is no objection to your making your Düreresque memoranda on grey or yellow paper, and touching or relieving them with white; only, do not depend much on your white touches, nor make the sketch for their sake.

116. Thirdly. When you have neither time for careful study nor for Düreresque detail, sketch the outline with pencil, then dash in the shadows with the brush boldly, trying to do as much as you possibly can at once,

and to get a habit of expedition and decision;
laying more colour again and again into the
tints as they dry, using every expedient
which your practice has suggested to you of
carrying out your chiaroscuro in the manage-
able and moist material, taking the colour
off here with the dry brush, scratching out
lights in it there with the wooden handle
of the brush, rubbing it in with your fingers,
drying it off with your sponge, &c. Then,
when the colour is in, take your pen and
mark the outline characters vigorously, in
the manner of the Liber Studiorum. This
kind of study is very convenient for carrying
away pieces of effect which depend not so
much on refinement as on complexity, strange
shapes of involved shadows, sudden effects
of sky, &c.; and it is most useful as a safeguard against any too servile or slow habits
which the minute copying may induce in
you; for although the endeavour to obtain
velocity merely for velocity's sake, and dash
for display's sake, is as baneful as it is des-
picable; there *are* a velocity and a dash
which not only are compatible with perfect
drawing, but obtain certain results which

cannot be had otherwise. And it is perfectly
safe for you to study occasionally for speed
and decision, while your continual course of
practice is such as to ensure your retaining
an accurate judgment and a tender touch.
Speed, under such circumstances, is rather
fatiguing than tempting; and you will find

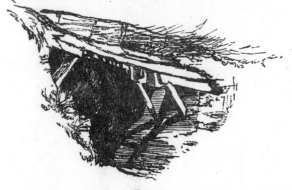

FIG. 21.

yourself always beguiled rather into elabora-
tion than negligence.

117. Fourthly. You will find it of great use,
whatever kind of landscape scenery you are
passing through, to get into the habit of
making memoranda of the shapes of shadows.
You will find that many objects of no essential

interest in themselves, and neither deserving
a finished study, nor a Düreresque one, may
yet become of singular value in consequence
of the fantastic shapes of their shadows; for
it happens often, in distant effect, that the

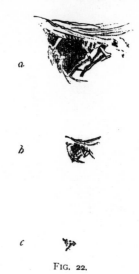

FIG. 22.

shadow is by much a more important element
than the substance.   Thus, in the Alpine
bridge, Fig. 21, seen within a few yards of it,
as in the figure, the arrangement of timbers
to which the shadows are owing is perceptible;

but at half a mile's distance, in bright sunlight,
the timbers would not be seen; and a good
painter's expression of the bridge would be
merely the large spot, and the crossed bars,
of pure grey; wholly without indication of
their cause, as in Fig. 22 a; and if we saw
it at still greater distances, it would appear,
as in Fig. 22 b and c, diminishing at last
to a strange, unintelligible, spider-like spot of
grey on the light hill-side. A perfectly great
painter, throughout his distances, continually
reduces his objects to these shadow abstracts;
and the singular, and to many persons un-
accountable, effect of the confused touches in
Turner's distances, is owing chiefly to this
thorough accuracy and intense meaning of
the shadow abstracts.

118. Studies of this kind are easily made,
when you are in haste, with an F. or HB.
pencil: it requires some hardness of the point
to ensure your drawing delicately enough when
the forms of the shadows are very subtle; they
are sure to be so somewhere, and are generally
so everywhere. The pencil is indeed a very
precious instrument after you are master of
the pen and brush, for the pencil, cunningly

K

used, is both, and will draw a line with the precision of the one and the gradation of the other; nevertheless, it is so unsatisfactory to see the sharp touches, on which the best of the detail depends, getting gradually deadened by time, or to find the places where force was wanted look shiny, and like a fire-grate, that I should recommend rather the steady use of the pen, or brush, and colour, whenever time admits of it; keeping only a small memorandum-book in the breast-pocket, with its well-cut, sheathed pencil, ready for notes on passing opportunities: but never being without this.

119. Thus much, then, respecting the manner in which you are at first to draw from Nature. But it may perhaps be serviceable to you, if I also note one or two points respecting your choice of subjects for study, and the best special methods of treating some of them; for one of by no means the least difficulties which you have at first to encounter is a peculiar instinct, common, as far as I have noticed, to all beginners, to fix on exactly the most unmanageable feature in the given scene. There are many things in every

landscape which can be drawn, if at all, only by the most accomplished artists; and I have noticed that it is nearly always these which a beginner will dash at; or, if not these, it will be something which, though pleasing to him in itself, is unfit for a picture, and in which, when he has drawn it, he will have little pleasure. As some slight protection against this evil genius of beginners, the following general warnings may be useful:

120. (1.) Do not draw things that you love, on account of their associations; or at least do not draw them because you love them; but merely when you cannot get anything else to draw. If you try to draw places that you love, you are sure to be always entangled amongst neat brick walls, iron railings, gravel walks, greenhouses, and quickset hedges; besides that you will be continually led into some endeavour to make your drawing pretty, or complete, which will be fatal to your progress. You need never hope to get on, if you are the least anxious that the drawing you are actually at work upon should look nice when it is done. All you have to care about is to make it *right*, and to learn as much in

doing it as possible. So then, though when you are sitting in your friend's parlour, or in your own, and have nothing else to do, you may draw anything that is there, for practice ; even the fire-irons or the pattern on the carpet : be sure that it *is* for practice, and not because it is a beloved carpet, or a friendly poker and tongs, nor because you wish to please your friend by drawing her room.

121. Also, never make presents of your drawings. Of course I am addressing you as a beginner—a time may come when your work will be precious to everybody ; but be resolute not to give it away till you know that it is worth something (as soon as it is worth anything you will know that it is so). If any one asks you for a present of a drawing, send them a couple of cakes of colour and a piece of Bristol board : those materials are, for the present, of more value in that form than if you had spread the one over the other.

The main reason for this rule is, however, that its observance will much protect you from the great danger of trying to make your drawings pretty.

122. (2.) Never, by choice, draw anything polished; especially if complicated in form. Avoid all brass rods and curtain ornaments, chandeliers, plate, glass, and fine steel. A shining knob of a piece of furniture does not matter if it comes in your way; but do not fret yourself if it will not look right, and choose only things that do not shine.

(3.) Avoid all very neat things. They are exceedingly difficult to draw, and very ugly when drawn. Choose rough, worn, and clumsy-looking things as much as possible; for instance, you cannot have a more difficult or profitless study than a newly painted Thames wherry, nor a better study than an old empty coal-barge, lying ashore at low tide: in general, everything that you think very ugly will be good for you to draw.

(4.) Avoid, as much as possible, studies in which one thing is seen through another. You will constantly find a thin tree standing before your chosen cottage, or between you and the turn of the river; its near branches all entangled with the distance. It is intensely difficult to represent this; and though, when the tree *is* there, you must not imaginarily cut it down, but do it as well as you can, yet always look for subjects that fall into definite masses, not into network; that is, rather for a cottage with a dark tree beside it, than for one with a thin tree in front of it, rather for a mass of wood, soft, blue, and rounded, than for a ragged copse, or confusion of intricate stems.

(5.) Avoid, as far as possible, country divided by hedges. Perhaps nothing in the whole compass of landscape is so utterly unpicturesque and unmanageable as the ordinary English patchwork of field and hedge, with trees dotted over it in independent spots, gnawed straight at the cattle line.

Still, do not be discouraged if you find you have chosen ill, and that the subject overmasters you. It is much better that it should, than that you should think you had entirely mastered *it*. But at first, and even for some time, you must be prepared for very discomfortable failure; which, nevertheless, will not be without some wholesome result.

123. As, however, I have told you what most definitely to avoid, I may, perhaps, help

you a little by saying what to seek. In general, all banks are beautiful things, and will reward work better than large landscapes. If you live in a lowland country, you must look for places where the ground is broken to the river's edges, with decayed posts, or roots of trees; or, if by great good luck there should be such things within your reach, for remnants of stone quays or steps, mossy mill-dams, &c. Nearly every other mile of road in chalk country will present beautiful bits of broken bank at its sides; better in form and colour than high chalk cliffs. In woods, one or two trunks, with the flowery ground below, are at once the richest and easiest kind of study: a not very thick trunk, say nine inches or a foot in diameter, with ivy running up it sparingly, is an easy, and always a rewarding subject.

124. Large nests of buildings in the middle distance are always beautiful, when drawn carefully, provided they are not modern rows of pattern cottages, or villas with Ionic and Doric porticoes. Any old English village, or cluster of farm-houses, drawn with all its ins and outs, and haystacks, and palings, is sure to

be lovely; much more a French one.   French landscape is generally as much superior to English as Swiss landscape is to French; in some respects, the French is incomparable. Such scenes as that avenue on the Seine, which I have recommended you to buy the engraving of, admit no rivalship in their expression of graceful rusticity and cheerful peace, and in the beauty of component lines.

In drawing villages, take great pains with the gardens; a rustic garden is in every way beautiful.   If you have time, draw all the rows of cabbages, and hollyhocks, and broken fences, and wandering eglantines, and bossy roses; you cannot have better practice, nor be kept by anything in purer thoughts.

Make intimate friends with all the brooks in your neighbourhood, and study them ripple by ripple.

Village churches in England are not often good subjects; there is a peculiar meanness about most of them and awkwardness of line. Old manor-houses are often pretty.   Ruins are usually, with us, too prim, and cathedrals too orderly.   I do not think there is a single cathedral in England from which it is possible

to obtain *one* subject for an impressive drawing.   There is always some discordant civility,
or jarring vergerism about them.

125. If you live in a mountain or hill country,
your only danger is redundance of subject. Be
resolved, in the first place, to draw a piece of
rounded rock, with its variegated lichens, quite
rightly, getting its complete roundings, and all
the patterns of the lichen in true local colour.
Till you can do this, it is of no use your thinking
of sketching among hills; but when once you
have done this, the forms of distant hills will
be comparatively easy.

126. When you have practised for a little
time from such of these subjects as may be
accessible to you, you will certainly find difficulties arising which will make you wish more
than ever for a master's help: these difficulties
will vary according to the character of your
own mind (one question occurring to one
person, and one to another), so that it is impossible to anticipate them all; and it would
make this too large a book if I answered all
that I *can* anticipate; you must be content to
work on, in good hope that Nature will, in her
own time, interpret to you much for herself;

that farther experience on your own part will make some difficulties disappear ; and that others will be removed by the occasional observation of such artists' work as may come in your way.   Nevertheless, I will not close this letter without a few general remarks, such as may be useful to you after you are somewhat advanced in power ; and these remarks may, I think, be conveniently arranged under three heads, having reference to the drawing of vegetation, water, and skies.

127. And, first, of vegetation.   You may think, perhaps, we have said enough about trees already ; yet if you have done as you were bid, and tried to draw them frequently enough, and carefully enough, you will be ready by this time to hear a little more of them. You will also recollect that we left our question, respecting the mode of expressing intricacy of leafage, partly unsettled in the first letter.   I left it so because I wanted you to learn the real structure of leaves, by drawing them for yourself, before I troubled you with the most subtle considerations as to method in drawing them.   And by this time, I imagine, you must have found out two principal things,

universal facts, about leaves ; namely, that they always, in the main tendencies of their lines, indicate a beautiful divergence of growth, according to the law of radiation, already referred to ;[1] and the second, that this divergence is never formal, but carried out with endless variety of individual line. I must now press both these facts on your attention a little farther.

128. You may, perhaps, have been surprised that I have not yet spoken of the works of J. D. Harding, especially if you happen to have met with the passages referring to them in Modern Painters, in which they are highly praised. They are deservedly praised, for they are the only works by a modern[2] draughtsman which express in any wise the energy of trees, and the laws of growth, of which we have been speaking. There are no lithographic sketches which, for truth of general character, obtained with little cost of time, at all rival Harding's. Calame, Robert, and the other lithographic landscape sketchers are altogether inferior in power, though sometimes a little deeper in meaning. But you must not take

[1] See the closing letter in this volume.   [2 In 1857.]

even Harding for a model, though you may use his works for occasional reference; and if you can afford to buy his Lessons on Trees,[1] it will be serviceable to you in various ways, and will at present help me to explain the point under consideration. And it is well that I should illustrate this point by reference to Harding's works, because their great influence on young students renders it desirable that their real character should be thoroughly understood.

129. You will find, first, in the titlepage of the Lessons on Trees, a pretty woodcut, in which the tree stems are drawn with great truth, and in a very interesting arrangement of lines. Plate 1 is not quite worthy of Mr. Harding, tending too much to make his pupil, at starting, think everything depends on black dots; still, the main lines are good, and very characteristic of tree growth. Then, in Plate 2, we come to the point at issue. The first examples in that plate are given to the pupil

[1] If you are not acquainted with Harding's works, (an unlikely supposition, considering their popularity,) and cannot meet with the one in question, the diagrams given here will enable you to understand all that is needful for our purposes.

that he may practise from them till his hand
gets into the habit of arranging lines freely
in a similar manner; and they are stated
by Mr. Harding to be universal in application; "all outlines expressive of foliage," he
says, "are but modifications of them." They
consist of groups of lines, more or less
resembling our Fig. 23 below; and the
characters especially insisted upon are, that
they "tend at their inner ends to a common
centre;" that "their ends terminate in [are
enclosed by] ovoid curves;" and that "the
outer ends are most emphatic."

130. Now, as thus
expressive of the great
laws of radiation and
enclosure, the main
principle of this method
of execution confirms,

FIG. 23.

in a very interesting way, our conclusions
respecting foliage composition. The reason of
the last rule, that the outer end of the line
is to be most emphatic, does not indeed at
first appear; for the line at one end of a
natural leaf is not more emphatic than the
line at the other: but ultimately, in Harding's

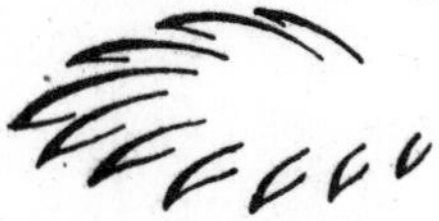

method, this darker part of the touch stands more or less for the shade at the outer extremity of the leaf mass; and, as Harding uses these touches, they express as much of tree character as any mere habit of touch *can* express. But, unfortunately, there is another law of tree growth, quite as fixed as the law of radiation, which this and all other conventional modes of execution wholly lose sight of. This second law is, that the radiating tendency shall be carried out only as a ruling spirit in reconcilement with perpetual individual caprice on the part of the separate leaves. So that the moment a touch is monotonous, it must be also false, the liberty of the leaf individually being just as essential a truth, as its unity of growth with its companions in the radiating group.

131. It does not matter how small or apparently symmetrical the cluster may be, nor how large or vague. You can hardly have a more formal one than *b* in Fig. 9, p. 84, nor a less formal one than this shoot of Spanish chestnut, shedding its leaves, Fig. 24; but in either of them, even the general reader, unpractised in any of the previously

recommended exercises, must see that there
are wandering lines mixed with the radiating
ones, and radiating lines with the wild ones :
and if he takes the pen, and tries to copy either
of these examples, he will find that neither
play of hand to left nor to right, neither a free
touch nor a firm touch, nor any learnable or

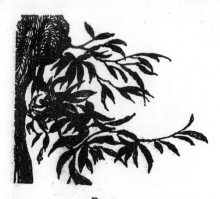

FIG. 24.

describable touch whatsoever, will enable him
to produce, currently, a resemblance of it ;
but that he must either draw it slowly or
give it up.   And (which makes the matter
worse still) though gathering the bough, and
putting it close to you, or seeing a piece of
near foliage against the sky, you may draw

the entire outline of the leaves, yet if the
spray has light upon it, and is ever so little
a way off, you will miss, as we have seen,
a point of a leaf here, and an edge there;
some of the surfaces will be confused by
glitter, and some spotted with shade; and if
you look carefully through this confusion for
the edges or dark stems which you really *can*
see and put only those down, the result will

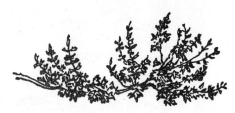

FIG. 25.

be neither like Fig. 9 nor Fig. 24, but such
an interrupted and puzzling piece of work as
Fig. 25.[1]

132. Now, it is in the perfect acknowledg-
ment and expression of these *three* laws
that all good drawing of landscape consists.

[1] I draw this figure (a young shoot of oak) in outline only,
it being impossible to express the refinements of shade in
distant foliage in a woodcut.

There is, first, the organic unity; the law, whether of radiation, or parallelism, or concurrent action, which rules the masses of herbs and trees, of rocks, and clouds, and waves; secondly, the individual liberty of the members subjected to these laws of unity; and, lastly, the mystery under which the separate character of each is more or less concealed.

I say, first, there must be observance of the ruling organic law. This is the first distinction between good artists and bad artists. Your common sketcher or bad painter puts his leaves on the trees as if they were moss tied to sticks; he cannot see the lines of action or growth; he scatters the shapeless clouds over his sky, not perceiving the sweeps of associated curves which the real clouds are following as they fly; and he breaks his mountain side into rugged fragments, wholly unconscious of the lines of force with which the real rocks have risen, or of the lines of couch in which they repose. On the contrary, it is the main delight of the great draughtsman to trace these laws of government; and his tendency to error is

L

always in the exaggeration of their authority rather than in its denial.

133. Secondly, I say, we have to show the individual character and liberty of the separate leaves, clouds, or rocks. And herein the great masters separate themselves finally from the inferior ones; for if the men of inferior genius ever express law at all, it is by the sacrifice of individuality. Thus, Salvator Rosa has great perception of the sweep of foliage and rolling of clouds, but never draws a single leaflet or mist wreath accurately. Similarly, Gainsborough, in his landscape, has great feeling for masses of form and harmony of colour; but in the detail gives nothing but meaningless touches; not even so much as the species of tree, much less the variety of its leafage, being ever discernible. Now, although both these expressions of government and individuality are essential to masterly work, the individuality is the *more* essential, and the more difficult of attainment; and, therefore, that attainment separates the great masters *finally* from the inferior ones. It is the more essential, because, in these matters of beautiful arrangement in

visible things, the same rules hold that hold in moral things. It is a lamentable and unnatural thing to see a number of men subject to no government, actuated by no ruling principle, and associated by no common affection : but it would be a more lamentable thing still, were it possible, to see a number of men so oppressed into assimilation as to have no more any individual hope or character, no differences in aim, no dissimilarities of passion, no irregularities of judgment; a society in which no man could help another, since none would be feebler than himself; no man admire another, since none would be stronger than himself; no man be grateful to another, since by none he could be relieved; no man reverence another, since by none he could be instructed; a society in which every soul would be as the syllable of a stammerer instead of the word of a speaker, in which every man would walk as in a frightful dream, seeing spectres of himself, in everlasting multiplication, gliding helplessly around him in a speechless darkness. Therefore it is that perpetual difference, play, and change in groups of form are more essential to them even than their being subdued by some great gathering law: the law is needful to them for their perfection and their power, but the difference is needful to them for their life.

134. And here it may be noted in passing, that, if you enjoy the pursuit of analogies and types, and have any ingenuity of judgment in discerning them, you may always accurately ascertain what are the noble characters in a piece of painting by merely considering what are the noble characters of man in his association with his fellows. What grace of manner and refinement of habit are in society, grace of line and refinement of form are in the association of visible objects. What advantage or harm there may be in sharpness, ruggedness, or quaintness in the dealings or conversations of men; precisely that relative degree of advantage or harm there is in them as elements of pictorial composition. What power is in liberty or relaxation to strengthen or relieve human souls; that power precisely in the same relative degree, play and laxity of line have to strengthen or refresh the expression of a picture. And what goodness or greatness

we can conceive to arise in companies of men, from chastity of thought, regularity of life, simplicity of custom, and balance of authority; precisely that kind of goodness and greatness may be given to a picture by the purity of its colour, the severity of its forms, and the symmetry of its masses.

135. You need not be in the least afraid of pushing these analogies too far. They cannot be pushed too far; they are so precise and complete, that the farther you pursue them, the clearer, the more certain, the more useful you will find them. They will not fail you in one particular, or in any direction of enquiry. There is no moral vice, no moral virtue, which has not its *precise* prototype in the art of painting; so that you may at your will illustrate the moral habit by the art, or the art by the moral habit. Affection and discord, fretfulness and quietness, feebleness and firmness, luxury and purity, pride and modesty, and all other such habits, and every conceivable modification and mingling of them, may be illustrated, with mathematical exactness, by conditions of line and colour; and not merely these definable vices and virtues, but also every conceivable

shade of human character and passion, from
the righteous or unrighteous majesty of the
king to the innocent or faultful simplicity of
the shepherd boy.

136. The pursuit of this subject belongs
properly, however, to the investigation of the
higher branches of composition, matters which
it would be quite useless to treat of in this
book ; and I only allude to them here, in order
that you may understand how the utmost
noblenesses of art are concerned in this minute
work, to which I have set you in your beginning of it.   For it is only by the closest
attention, and the most noble execution, that
it is possible to express these varieties of
individual character, on which all excellence
of portraiture depends, whether of masses of
mankind, or of groups of leaves.

137. Now you will be able to understand,
among other matters, wherein consists the
excellence, and wherein the shortcoming, of
the tree-drawing of Harding.   It is excellent
in so far as it fondly observes, with more truth
than any other work of the kind, the great
laws of growth and action in trees : it fails,
—and observe, not in a minor, but in the

principal point, — because it cannot rightly
render any one individual detail or incident of
foliage.   And in this it fails, not from mere
carelessness or incompletion, but of necessity;
the true drawing of detail being for evermore
impossible to a hand which has contracted a
habit of execution.   The noble draughtsman
draws a leaf, and stops, and says calmly, —
That leaf is of such and such a character; I
will give him a friend who will entirely suit
him: then he considers what his friend ought
to be, and having determined, he draws his
friend.   This process may be as quick as
lightning when the master is great—one of the
sons of the giants; or it may be slow and
timid: but the process is always gone through;
no touch or form is ever added to another by
a good painter without a mental determination
and affirmation.   But when the hand has got
into a habit, leaf No. 1 necessitates leaf No. 2;
you cannot stop, your hand is as a horse
with the bit in its teeth; or rather is, for the
time, a machine, throwing out leaves to order
and pattern, all alike.   You must stop that
hand of yours, however painfully; make it
understand that it is not to have its own way

any more, that it shall never more slip from
one touch to another without orders; otherwise it is not you who are the master, but
your fingers.   You may therefore study Harding's drawing, and take pleasure in it;[1] and
you may properly admire the dexterity which
applies the habit of the hand so well, and
produces results on the whole so satisfactory:
but you must never copy it; otherwise your
progress will be at once arrested.   The utmost
you can ever hope to do would be a sketch in
Harding's manner, but of far inferior dexterity;
for he has given his life's toil to gain his dexterity, and you, I suppose, have other things
to work at besides drawing.   You would also
incapacitate yourself from ever understanding
what truly great work was, or what Nature
was; but, by the earnest and complete study
of facts, you will gradually come to understand
the one and love the other more and more,
whether you can draw well yourself or not.

138. I have yet to say a few words

---

[1] His lithographic sketches, those for instance in the Park
and the Forest, and his various lessons on foliage, possess
greater merit than the more ambitious engravings in his
Principles and Practice of Art. There are many useful
remarks, however, dispersed through this latter work.

respecting the third law above stated, that
of mystery; the law, namely, that nothing is
ever seen perfectly, but only by fragments,
and under various conditions of obscurity.[1]
This last fact renders the visible objects of
Nature complete as a type of the human
nature. We have, observe, first, Subordination; secondly, Individuality; lastly, and this
not the least essential character, Incompre-
hensibility; a perpetual lesson, in every ser-
rated point and shining vein which escapes or
deceives our sight among the forest leaves,
how little we may hope to discern clearly, or
judge justly, the rents and veins of the human
heart; how much of all that is round us, in
men's actions or spirits, which we at first
think we understand, a closer and more loving watchfulness would show to be full of
mystery, never to be either fathomed or with-
drawn.

139. The expression of this final character
in landscape has never been completely reached
by any except Turner; nor can you hope to

---

[1] On this law you do well, if you can get access to it, to
look at the fourth chapter of the fourth volume of Modern
Painters.

reach it at all until you have given much time
to the practice of art.   Only try always when
you are sketching any object with a view to
completion in light and shade, to draw only

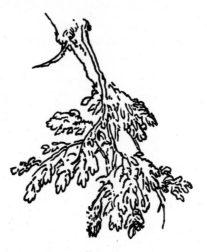

FIG. 26.

those parts of it which you really see definitely; preparing for the after development
of the forms by chiaroscuro. It is this preparation by isolated touches for a future arrangement of superimposed light and shade which
renders the etchings of the Liber Studiorum

so inestimable as examples, and so peculiar.
The character exists more or less in them
exactly in proportion to the pains that Turner
has taken. Thus the Æsacus and Hesperie
was wrought out with the greatest possible
care; and the principal branch on the near
tree is etched as in Fig. 26. The work looks
at first like a scholar's instead of a master's;
but when the light and shade are added, every
touch falls into its place, and a perfect expression of grace and complexity results. Nay,
even before the light and shade are added,
you ought to be able to see that these irregular
and broken lines, especially where the expression is given of the way the stem loses itself
in the leaves, are more true than the monotonous though graceful leaf-drawing which,
before Turner's time, had been employed, even
by the best masters, in their distant masses.
Fig. 27 is sufficiently characteristic of the
manner of the old woodcuts after Titian; in
which, you see, the leaves are too much of one
shape, like bunches of fruit; and the boughs
too completely seen, besides being somewhat
soft and leathery in aspect, owing to the want
of angles in their outline. By great men like

Titian, this somewhat conventional structure was only given in haste to distant masses; and their exquisite delineation of the foreground, kept their conventionalism from degeneracy: but in the drawings of the Carracci and other derivative masters, the conventionalism prevails everywhere, and sinks gradually into scrawled work, like Fig. 28, about the

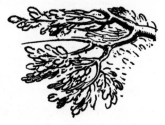

FIG. 27.

worst which it is possible to get into the habit of using, though an ignorant person might perhaps suppose it more "free," and therefore better than Fig. 26. Note also, that in noble outline drawing, it does not follow that a bough is wrongly drawn, because it looks contracted unnaturally somewhere, as in Fig. 26, just above the foliage. Very often the muscular action which is to be expressed by the line runs into the middle of the branch, and the actual outline of the branch at that place may be dimly seen, or not at all; and it is then only by the future shade that its actual

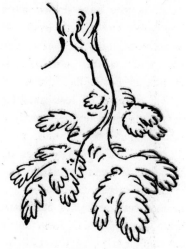

FIG. 28.

shape, or the cause of its disappearance, will be indicated.

140. One point more remains to be noted about trees, and I have done. In the minds of our ordinary water-colour artists a distant tree seems only to be conceived as a flat

green blot, grouping pleasantly with other masses, and giving cool colour to the landscape, but differing no wise, in texture, from the blots of other shapes which these painters use to express stones, or water, or figures. But as soon as you have drawn trees carefully a little while, you will be impressed, and impressed more strongly the better you draw them, with the idea of their *softness* of surface. A distant tree is not a flat and even piece of colour, but a more or less globular mass of a downy or bloomy texture, partly passing into a misty vagueness. I find, practically, this lovely softness of far-away trees the most difficult of all characters to reach, because it cannot be got by mere scratching or roughening the surface, but is always associated with such delicate expressions of form and growth as are only imitable by very careful drawing. The penknife passed lightly *over* this careful drawing will do a good deal; but you must accustom yourself, from the beginning, to aim much at this softness in the lines of the drawing itself, by crossing them delicately, and more or less effacing and confusing the edges. You must invent, according to the character

of tree, various modes of execution adapted
to express its texture; but always keep this
character of softness in your mind, and in
your scope of aim; for in most landscapes it
is the intention of Nature that the tenderness
and transparent infinitude of her foliage should
be felt, even at the far distance, in the most
distinct opposition to the solid masses and flat
surfaces of rocks or buildings.

141. II. We were, in the second place, to
consider a little the modes of representing
water, of which important feature of landscape I have hardly said anything yet.

Water is expressed, in common drawings,
by conventional lines, whose horizontality is
supposed to convey the idea of its surface.
In paintings, white dashes or bars of light
are used for the same purpose.

But these and all other such expedients
are vain and absurd. A piece of calm
water always contains a picture in itself, an
exquisite reflection of the objects above it.
If you give the time necessary to draw these
reflections, disturbing them here and there
as you see the breeze or current disturb

them, you will get the effect of the water;
but if you have not patience to draw the
reflections, no expedient will give you a true
effect. The picture in the pool needs nearly
as much delicate drawing as the picture above
the pool; except only that if there be the
least motion on the water, the horizontal lines
of the images will be diffused and broken,
while the vertical ones will remain decisive,
and the oblique ones decisive in proportion
to their steepness.

142. A few close studies will soon teach
you this: the only thing you need to be told
is to watch carefully the lines of disturbance
on the surface, as when a bird swims across
it, or a fish rises, or the current plays round
a stone, reed, or other obstacle. Take the
greatest pains to get the *curves* of these lines
true; the whole value of your careful drawing of the reflections may be lost by your
admitting a single false curve of ripple from
a wild duck's breast. And (as in other
subjects) if you are dissatisfied with your
result, always try for more unity and delicacy: if your reflections are only soft and
gradated enough, they are nearly sure to

give you a pleasant effect.[1] When you are
taking pains, work the softer reflections,
where they are drawn out by motion in the
water, with touches as nearly horizontal as
may be; but when you are in a hurry, indicate the place and play of the images with
vertical lines. The actual construction of a
calm elongated reflection is with horizontal
lines: but it is often impossible to draw the
descending shades delicately enough with a
horizontal touch; and it is best always when
you are in a hurry, and sometimes when you
are not, to use the vertical touch. When
the ripples are large, the reflections become
shaken, and must be drawn with bold undulatory descending lines.

143. I need not, I should think, tell you
that it is of the greatest possible importance
to draw the curves of the shore rightly.
Their perspective is, if not more subtle, at
least more stringent than that of any other
lines in Nature. It will not be detected by
the general observer, if you miss the curve
of a branch, or the sweep of a cloud, or the

---

[1] See Note 3 in Appendix I.

M

perspective of a building;[1] but every intelligent spectator will feel the difference between
a rightly-drawn bend of shore or shingle, and
a false one. *Absolutely* right, in difficult river
perspectives seen from heights, I believe
no one but Turner ever has been yet; and
observe, there is NO rule for them. To de-
velope the curve mathematically would require
a knowledge of the exact quantity of water in
the river, the shape of its bed, and the hardness of the rock or shore; and even with
these data, the problem would be one which
no mathematician could solve but approxi-
matively. The instinct of the eye can do it;
nothing else.

144. If, after a little study from Nature,
you get puzzled by the great differences between the aspect of the reflected image and
that of the object casting it; and if you wish
to know the law of reflection, it is simply
this: Suppose all the objects above the water
actually reversed (not in appearance, but in

[1] The student may hardly at first believe that the perspective of buildings is of little consequence; but he will find
it so ultimately. See the remarks on this point in the
Preface.

fact) beneath the water, and precisely the same in form and in relative position, only all topsy-turvy. Then, whatever you could see, from the place in which you stand, of the solid objects so reversed under the water, you will see in the reflection, always in the true perspective of the solid objects so reversed.

If you cannot quite understand this in looking at water, take a mirror, lay it horizontally on the table, put some books and papers upon it, and draw them and their reflections; moving them about, and watching how their reflections alter, and chiefly how their reflected colours and shades differ from their own colours and shades, by being brought into other oppositions. This difference in chiaroscuro is a more important character in water-painting than mere difference in form.

145. When you are drawing shallow or muddy water, you will see shadows on the bottom, or on the surface, continually modifying the reflections; and in a clear mountain stream, the most wonderful complications of effect resulting from the shadows and reflections of the stones in it, mingling with the

aspect of the stones themselves seen through
the water.   Do not be frightened at the complexity; but, on the other hand, do not hope
to render it hastily.   Look at it well, making
out everything that you see, and distinguish-
ing each component part of the effect.   There
will be, first, the stones seen through the
water, distorted always by refraction, so that,
if the general structure of the stone shows
straight parallel lines above the water, you
may be sure they will be bent where they
enter it; then the reflection of the part of the
stone above the water crosses and interferes
with the part that is seen through it, so that
you can hardly tell which is which; and
wherever the reflection is darkest, you will
see through the water best,[1] and *vice versâ*.
Then the real shadow of the stone crosses
both these images, and where that shadow
falls, it makes the water more reflective, and
where the sunshine falls, you will see more of
the surface of the water, and of any dust or
motes that may be floating on it: but whether
you are to see, at the same spot, most of the

---

[1] See Note 4 in Appendix I.

bottom of the water, or of the reflection of the objects above, depends on the position of the eye. The more you look down into the water, the better you see objects through it; the more you look along it, the eye being low, the more you see the reflection of objects above it. Hence the colour of a given space of surface in a stream will entirely change while you stand still in the same spot, merely as you stoop or raise your head; and thus the colours with which water is painted are an indication of the position of the spectator, and connected inseparably with the perspective of the shores. The most beautiful of all results that I know in mountain streams is when the water is shallow, and the stones at the bottom are rich reddish-orange and black, and the water is seen at an angle which exactly divides the visible colours between those of the stones and that of the sky, and the sky is of clear, full blue. The resulting purple, obtained by the blending of the blue and the orange-red, broken by the play of innumerable gradations in the stones, is indescribably lovely.

146. All this seems complicated enough

already; but if there be a strong colour in
the clear water itself, as of green or blue
in the Swiss lakes, all these phenomena are
doubly involved; for the darker reflections
now become of the colour of the water. The
reflection of a black gondola, for instance, at
Venice, is never black, but pure dark green.
And, farther, the colour of the water itself is
of three kinds : one, seen on the surface, is a
kind of milky bloom; the next is seen where
the waves let light through them, at their
edges; and the third, shown as a change of
colour on the objects seen through the water.
Thus, the same wave that makes a white
object look of a clear blue, when seen
through it, will take a red or violet-coloured
bloom on its surface, and will be made
pure emerald green by transmitted sunshine
through its edges. With all this, however,
you are not much concerned at present, but
I tell it you partly as a preparation for what
we have afterwards to say about colour, and
partly that you may approach lakes and
streams with reverence,[1] and study them as

---

[1] See Note 5 in Appendix I.

carefully as other things, not hoping to express them by a few horizontal dashes of
white, or a few tremulous blots.[1]   Not but
that much may be done by tremulous blots,
when you know precisely what you mean by
them, as you will see by many of the Turner
sketches, which are now framed at the
National Gallery; but you must have painted
water many and many a day—yes, and all
day long—before you can hope to do anything like those.

147. III. Lastly.   You may perhaps wonder
why, before passing to the clouds, I say
nothing special about *ground*.[2]   But there is
too much to be said about that to admit of

[1] It is a useful piece of study to dissolve some Prussian
blue in water, so as to make the liquid definitely blue : fill a
large white basin with the solution, and put anything you
like to float on it, or lie in it ; walnut shells, bits of wood,
leaves of flowers, &c.   Then study the effects of the reflections, and of the stems of the flowers or submerged portions
of the floating objects, as they appear through the blue
liquid ; noting especially how, as you lower your head and
look along the surface, you see the reflections clearly ; and
how, as you raise your head, you lose the reflections, and
see the submerged stems clearly.

[2] Respecting Architectural Drawing, see the notice of the
works of Prout in the Appendix.

my saying it here.   You will find the principal laws of its structure examined at length
in the fourth volume of Modern Painters ; and
if you can get that volume, and copy carefully Plate 21, which I have etched after
Turner with great pains, it will give you as
much help as you need in the linear expression of ground-surface.   Strive to get
the retirement and succession of masses in
irregular ground : much may be done in this
way by careful watching of the perspective
diminutions of its herbage, as well as by contour ; and much also by shadows.   If you
draw the shadows of leaves and tree trunks
on any undulating ground with entire care-
fulness, you will be surprised to find how
much they explain of the form and distance
of the earth on which they fall.

148. Passing then to skies, note that there
is this great peculiarity about sky subject, as
distinguished from earth subject ; — that the
clouds, not being much liable to man's interference, are always beautifully arranged.   You
cannot be sure of this in any other features of
landscape.   The rock on which the effect of
a mountain scene especially depends is always

precisely that which the roadmaker blasts or the landlord quarries; and the spot of green which Nature left with a special purpose by her dark forest sides, and finished with her most delicate grasses, is always that which the farmer ploughs or builds upon. But the clouds, though we can hide them with smoke, and mix them with poison, cannot be quarried nor built over, and they are always therefore gloriously arranged; so gloriously, that unless you have notable powers of memory you need not hope to approach the effect of any sky that interests you. For both its grace and its glow depend upon the united influence of every cloud within its compass: they all move and burn together in a marvellous harmony; not a cloud of them is out of its appointed place, or fails of its part in the choir: and if you are not able to recollect (which in the case of a complicated sky it is impossible you should) precisely the form and position of all the clouds at a given moment, you cannot draw the sky at all; for the clouds will not fit if you draw one part of them three or four minutes before another.

149. You must try therefore to help what

memory you have, by sketching at the utmost
possible speed the whole range of the clouds;
marking, by any shorthand or symbolic work
you can hit upon, the peculiar character of
each, as transparent, or fleecy, or linear, or
undulatory; giving afterwards such completion to the parts as your recollection will
enable you to do.   This, however, only when
the sky is interesting from its general aspect;
at other times, do not try to draw all the
sky, but a single cloud: sometimes a round
cumulus will stay five or six minutes quite
steady enough to let you mark out his principal masses; and one or two white or
crimson lines which cross the sunrise will
often stay without serious change for as long.
And in order to be the readier in drawing
them, practise occasionally drawing lumps of
cotton, which will teach you better than any
other stable thing the kind of softness there
is in clouds.   For you will find when you
have made a few genuine studies of sky, and
then look at any ancient or modern painting,
that ordinary artists have always fallen into
one of two faults: either, in rounding the
clouds, they make them as solid and hard-

edged as a heap of stones tied up in a sack, or they represent them not as rounded at all, but as vague wreaths of mist or flat lights in the sky; and think they have done enough in leaving a little white paper between dashes of blue, or in taking an irregular space out with the sponge. Now clouds are not as solid as flour-sacks; but, on the other hand, they are neither spongy nor flat. They are definite and very beautiful forms of sculptured mist; sculptured is a perfectly accurate word; they are not more *drifted* into form than they are *carved* into form, the warm air around them cutting them into shape by absorbing the visible vapour beyond certain limits; hence their angular and fantastic outlines, as different from a swollen, spherical, or globular formation, on the one hand, as from that of flat films or shapeless mists on the other. And the worst of all is, that while these forms are difficult enough to draw on any terms, especially considering that they never stay quiet, they must be drawn also at greater disadvantage of light and shade than any others, the force of light in clouds being wholly unattainable by art; so that if we

put shade enough to express their form as
positively as it is expressed in reality, we
must make them painfully too dark on the
dark sides. Nevertheless, they are so beautiful, if you in the least succeed with them,
that you will hardly, I think, lose courage.

150. Outline them often with the pen, as
you can catch them here and there; one of
the chief uses of doing this will be, not so
much the memorandum so obtained, as the
lesson you will get respecting the softness
of the cloud-outlines. You will always find
yourself at a loss to see where the outline
really is; and when drawn it will always look
hard and false, and will assuredly be either
too round or too square, however often you
alter it, merely passing from the one fault to
the other and back again, the real cloud striking an inexpressible mean between roundness
and squareness in all its coils or battlements.
I speak at present, of course, only of the
cumulus cloud: the lighter wreaths and flakes
of the upper sky cannot be outlined;—they
can only be sketched, like locks of hair, by
many lines of the pen. Firmly developed
bars of cloud on the horizon are in general

easy enough, and may be drawn with decision. When you have thus accustomed yourself a little to the placing and action of clouds, try to work out their light and shade, just as carefully as you do that of other things, looking exclusively for examples of treatment to the vignettes in Rogers's Italy and Poems, and to the Liber Studiorum, unless you have access to some examples of Turner's own work. No other artist ever yet drew the sky: even Titian's clouds, and Tintoret's, are conventional. The clouds in the " Ben Arthur," "Source of Arveron," and "Calais Pier," are among the best of Turner's storm studies; and of the upper clouds, the vignettes to Rogers's Poems furnish as many examples as you need.

151. And now, as our first lesson was taken from the sky, so, for the present, let our last be. I do not advise you to be in any haste to master the contents of my next letter. If you have any real talent for drawing, you will take delight in the discoveries of natural loveliness, which the studies I have already proposed will lead you into, among the fields and hills; and be assured that the more

quietly and single-heartedly you take each
step in the art, the quicker, on the whole,
will your progress be. I would rather, indeed,
have discussed the subjects of the following
letter at greater length, and in a separate work
addressed to more advanced students ; but as
there are one or two things to be said on
composition which may set the young artist's
mind somewhat more at rest, or furnish him
with defence from the urgency of ill-advisers,
I will glance over the main heads of the
matter here ; trusting that my doing so may
not beguile you, my dear reader, from your
serious work, or lead you to think me, in
occupying part of this book with talk not
altogether relevant to it, less entirely or

            Faithfully yours,

                    J. RUSKIN.

LETTER III.

ON COLOUR AND COMPOSITION.

152. MY DEAR READER,—If you have been obedient, and have hitherto done all that I have told you, I trust it has not been without much subdued remonstrance, and some serious vexation. For I should be sorry if, when you were led by the course of your study to observe closely such things as are beautiful in colour, you had not longed to paint them, and felt considerable difficulty in complying with your restriction to the use of black, or blue, or grey. You *ought* to love colour, and to think nothing quite beautiful or perfect without it ; and if you really do love it, for its own sake, and are not merely desirous to colour because you think painting a finer thing than drawing, there is some chance you may colour well. Nevertheless, you need not hope ever to produce anything more than pleasant helps to memory, or

useful and suggestive sketches in colour, unless you mean to be wholly an artist. You may, in the time which other vocations leave at your disposal, produce finished, beautiful, and masterly drawings in light and shade. But to colour well, requires your life. It cannot be done cheaper. The difficulty of doing right is increased—not twofold nor threefold, but a thousandfold, and more—by the addition of colour to your work. For the chances are more than a thousand to one against your being right both in form and colour with a given touch : it is difficult enough to be right in form, if you attend to that only ; but when you have to attend, at the same moment, to a much more subtle thing than the form, the difficulty is strangely increased,—and multiplied almost to infinity by this great fact, that, while form is absolute, so that you can say at the moment you draw any line that it is either right or wrong, colour is wholly *relative*. Every hue throughout your work is altered by every touch that you add in other places; so that what was warm a minute ago, becomes cold when you have put a hotter colour in another place, and what was in harmony when you left it, becomes discordant as you set other colours beside it; so that every touch must be laid, not with a view to its effect at the time, but with a view to its effect in futurity, the result upon it of all that is afterwards to be done being previously considered. You may easily understand that, this being so, nothing but the devotion of life, and great genius besides, can make a colourist.

153. But though you cannot produce finished coloured drawings of any value, you may give yourself much pleasure, and be of great use to other people, by occasionally sketching with a view to colour only; and preserving distinct statements of certain colour facts—as that the harvest moon at rising was of such and such a red, and surrounded by clouds of such and such a rosy grey; that the mountains at evening were in truth so deep in purple; and the waves by the boat's side were indeed of that incredible green. This only, observe, if you have an eye for colour; but you may presume that you have this, if you enjoy colour.

154. And, though of course you should always give as much form to your subject as your attention to its colour will admit of, remember that

N

the whole value of what you are about depends, in a coloured sketch, on the colour merely.   If the colour is wrong, everything is wrong : just as, if you are singing, and sing false notes, it does not matter how true the words are.   If you sing at all, you must sing sweetly ; and if you colour at all, you must colour rightly.   Give up all the form, rather than the slightest part of the colour : just as, if you felt yourself in danger of a false note, you would give up the word, and sing a meaningless sound, if you felt that so you could save the note.   Never mind though your houses are all tumbling down,—though your clouds are mere blots, and your trees mere knobs, and your sun and moon like crooked sixpences,—so only that trees, clouds, houses, and sun or moon, are of the right colours.   Of course, the discipline you have gone through will enable you to hint something of form, even in the fastest sweep of the brush ; but do not let the thought of form hamper you in the least, when you begin to make coloured memoranda.   If you want the form of the subject, draw it in black and white.   If you want its colour, take its colour, and be sure you *have* it, and not a spurious, treacherous, half-measured piece of mutual concession, with the colours all wrong, and the forms still anything but right.   It is best to get into the habit of considering the coloured work merely as supplementary to your other studies; making your careful drawings of the subject first, and then a coloured memorandum separately, as shapeless as you like, but faithful in hue, and entirely minding its own business. This principle, however, bears chiefly on large and distant subjects: in foregrounds and near studies, the colour cannot be had without a good deal of definition of form.   For if you do not map the mosses on the stones accurately, you will not have the right quantity of colour in each bit of moss pattern, and then none of the colours will look right; but it always simplifies the work much if you are clear as to your point of aim, and satisfied, when necessary, to fail of all but that.

155. Now, of course, if I were to enter into detail respecting colouring, which is the beginning and end of a painter's craft, I should need to make this a work in three volumes instead of three letters, and to illustrate it in the costliest way.   I only hope, at present, to set

you pleasantly and profitably to work, leaving you, within the tethering of certain leading-strings, to gather what advantages you can from the works of art of which every year brings a greater number within your reach;— and from the instruction which, every year, our rising artists will be more ready to give kindly, and better able to give wisely.

156. And, first, of materials. Use hard cake colours, not moist colours: grind a sufficient quantity of each on your palette every morning, keeping a separate plate, large and deep, for colours to be used in broad washes, and wash both plate and palette every evening, so as to be able always to get good and pure colour when you need it; and force yourself into cleanly and orderly habits about your colours. The two best colourists of modern times, Turner and Rossetti,[1] afford us, I am sorry to say, no

---

[1] I give Rossetti this preëminence, because, though the leading Pre-Raphaelites have all about equal power over colour in the abstract, Rossetti and Holman Hunt are distinguished above the rest for rendering colour under effects of light; and of these two, Rossetti composes with richer fancy, and with a deeper sense of beauty, Hunt's stern realism leading him continually into harshness. Rossetti's carelessness, to do him justice, is only in water-colour, never in oil.

confirmation of this precept by their practice. Turner was, and Rossetti is, as slovenly in all their procedures as men can well be; but the result of this was, with Turner, that the colours have altered in all his pictures, and in many of his drawings; and the result of it with Rossetti is, that though his colours are safe, he has sometimes to throw aside work that was half done, and begin over again. William Hunt, of the Old Water-colour, is very neat in his practice; so, I believe, is Mulready; so is John Lewis; and so are the leading Pre-Raphaelites, Rossetti only excepted. And there can be no doubt about the goodness of the advice, if it were only for this reason, that the more particular you are about your colours the more you will get into a deliberate and methodical habit in using them, and all true speed in colouring comes of this deliberation.

157. Use Chinese white, well ground, to mix with your colours in order to pale them, instead of a quantity of water. You will thus be able to shape your masses more quietly, and play the colours about with more ease; they will not damp your paper so much, and you will be able to go on continually, and lay forms of

passing cloud and other fugitive or delicately shaped lights, otherwise unattainable except by time.

158. This mixing of white with the pigments, so as to render them opaque, constitutes body-colour drawing as opposed to transparent-colour drawing, and you will, perhaps, have it often said to you that this body-colour is "illegitimate." It is just as legitimate as oil-painting, being, so far as handling is concerned, the same process, only without its uncleanliness, its unwholesomeness, or its inconvenience; for oil will not dry quickly, nor carry safely, nor give the same effects of atmosphere without tenfold labour. And if you hear it said that the body-colour looks chalky or opaque, and, as is very likely, think so yourself, be yet assured of this, that though certain effects of glow and transparencies of gloom are not to be reached without transparent colour, those glows and glooms are *not* the noblest aim of art. After many years' study of the various results of fresco and oil painting in Italy, and of body-colour and transparent colour in England, I am now entirely convinced that the greatest things that are to be done in art must be done in dead

colour.   The habit of depending on varnish
or on lucid tints for transparency, makes the
painter comparatively lose sight of the nobler
translucence which is obtained by breaking
various colours amidst each other : and even
when, as by Correggio, exquisite play of hue is
joined with exquisite transparency, the delight
in the depth almost always leads the painter into
mean and false chiaroscuro ; it leads him to like
dark backgrounds instead of luminous ones,[1]

---

[1] All the degradation of art which was brought about,
after the rise of the Dutch school, by asphaltum, yellow
varnish, and brown trees would have been prevented, if
only painters had been forced to work in dead colour.   Any
colour will do for some people, if it is browned and shining ;
but fallacy in dead colour is detected on the instant.   I even
believe that whenever a painter begins to *wish* that he
could touch any portion of his work with gum, he is going
wrong.

It is necessary, however, in this matter, carefully to distinguish between translucency and lustre.   Translucency,
though, as I have said above, a dangerous temptation, is,
in its place, beautiful ; but lustre or *shininess* is always, in
painting, a defect.   Nay, one of my best painter-friends (the
"best" being understood to attach to both divisions of
that awkward compound word,) tried the other day to per-
suade me that lustre was an ignobleness in anything ; and it
was only the fear of treason to ladies' eyes, and to mountain
streams, and to morning dew, which kept me from yielding
the point to him.   One is apt always to generalise too quickly
in such matters ; but there can be no question that lustre is
destructive of loveliness in colour, as it is of intelligibility in

and to enjoy, in general, quality of colour more than grandeur of composition, and confined light rather than open sunshine : so that the really greatest thoughts of the greatest men have always, so far as I remember, been reached in dead colour, and the noblest oil pictures of Tintoret and Veronese are those which are likest frescoes.

159. Besides all this, the fact is, that though sometimes a little chalky and coarse-looking body-colour is, in a sketch, infinitely liker Nature than transparent colour : the bloom and mist of distance are accurately and instantly represented by the film of opaque blue (*quite* accurately, I think, by nothing else); and for ground, rocks, and buildings, the earthy and solid surface is, of course, always truer than the most finished and carefully wrought work in transparent tints can ever be.

160. Against one thing, however, I must steadily caution you. All kinds of colour are equally illegitimate, if you think they will allow you to alter at your pleasure, or blunder at your

form. Whatever may be the pride of a young beauty in the knowledge that her eyes shine (though perhaps even eyes are most beautiful in dimness), she would be sorry if her cheeks did ; and which of us would wish to polish a rose ?

ease.   There is *no* vehicle or method of colour
which admits of alteration or repentance; you
must be right at once, or never; and you might
as well hope to catch a rifle bullet in your hand,
and put it straight, when it was going wrong,
as to recover a tint once spoiled.   The secret
of all good colour in oil, water, or anything
else, lies primarily in that sentence spoken to me
by Mulready: "Know what you have to do."
The process may be a long one, perhaps: you
may have to ground with one colour; to touch it
with fragments of a second; to crumble a third
into the interstices; a fourth into the interstices
of the third; to glaze the whole with a fifth; and
to reinforce in points with a sixth: but whether
you have one, or ten, or twenty processes to go
through, you must go *straight* through them
knowingly and foreseeingly all the way; and if
you get the thing once wrong, there is no hope
for you but in washing or scraping boldly down
to the white ground, and beginning again.

161. The drawing in body-colour will tend to
teach you all this, more than any other method,
and above all it will prevent you from falling into
the pestilent habit of sponging to get texture;
a trick which has nearly ruined our modern

water-colour school of art. There are sometimes places in which a skilful artist will roughen his paper a little to get certain conditions of dusty colour with more ease than he could otherwise ; and sometimes a skilfully rased piece of paper will, in the midst of transparent tints, answer nearly the purpose of chalky body-colour in representing the surfaces of rocks or building. But artifices of this kind are always treacherous in a tyro's hands, tempting him to trust in them : and you had better always work on white or grey paper as smooth as silk ; [1] and never disturb the surface of your colour or paper, except finally to scratch out the very highest lights if you are using transparent colours.

162. I have said above that body-colour drawing will teach you the use of colour better than working with merely transparent tints ; but this is not because the process is an easier one, but because it is a more complete one, and also because it involves some working with

[1] But not shiny or greasy. Bristol board, or hot-pressed imperial, or grey paper that feels slightly adhesive to the hand, is best. Coarse, gritty, and sandy papers are fit only for blotters and blunderers ; no good draughtsman would lay a line on them. Turner worked much on a thin tough paper, dead in surface ; rolling up his sketches in tight bundles that would go deep into his pockets.

transparent tints in the best way. You are not
to think that because you use body-colour you
may make any kind of mess that you like, and
yet get out of it. But you are to avail yourself of the characters of your material, which
enable you most nearly to imitate the processes
of Nature.   Thus, suppose you have a red
rocky cliff to sketch, with blue clouds floating
over it. You paint your cliff first firmly, then
take your blue, mixing it to such a tint (and
here is a great part of the skill needed) that
when it is laid over the red, in the thickness
required for the effect of the mist, the warm
rock-colour showing through the blue cloud-
colour, may bring it to exactly the hue you want
(your upper tint, therefore, must be mixed colder
than you want it); then you lay it on, varying
it as you strike it, getting the forms of the mist
at once, and, if it be rightly done, with exquisite
quality of colour, from the warm tint's showing
through and between the particles of the other.
When it is dry, you may add a little colour
to retouch the edges where they want shape, or
heighten the lights where they want roundness,
or put another tone over the whole: but
you can take none away. If you touch or

disturb the surface, or by any untoward acci-
dent mix the under and upper colours together,
all is lost irrecoverably.   Begin your drawing
from the ground again if you like, or throw it
into the fire if you like.   But do not waste time
in trying to mend it.[1]

163. This discussion of the relative merits of
transparent and opaque colour has, however,
led us a little beyond the point where we
should have begun ; we must go back to our
palette, if you please.   Get a cake of each of
the hard colours named in the note below[2] and

[1] I insist upon this unalterability of colour the more
because I address you as a beginner, or an amateur : a great
artist can sometimes get out of a difficulty with credit, or repent without confession.   Yet even Titian's alterations usually
show as stains on his work.

[2] It is, I think, a piece of affectation to try to work with
few colours : it saves time to have enough tints prepared
without mixing, and you may at once allow yourself these
twenty-four.   If you arrange them in your colour-box in the
order I have set them down, you will always easily put your
finger on the one you want.

Cobalt	Smalt	Antwerp blue	Prussian blue
Black	Gamboge	Emerald green	Hooker's green
Lemon yellow	Cadmium yellow	Yellow ochre	Roman ochre
Raw sienna	Burnt sienna	Light red	Indian red
Mars orange	Extract of ver- milion	Carmine	Violet carmine
Brown madder	Burnt umber	Vandyke brown	Sepia

Antwerp blue and Prussian blue are not very permanent

try experiments on their simple combinations,
by mixing each colour with every other. If you
like to do it in an orderly way, you may prepare a squared piece of pasteboard, and put the
pure colours in columns at the top and side ;
the mixed tints being given at the intersections,
thus (the letters standing for colours) :

	b	c	d	e	f	&c.
a	a b	a c	a d	a e	a f	
b		b c	b d	b e	b f	
c		—	c d	c e	c f	
d	—	—	—	d e	d f	
e		—	—		e f	
&c.						

This will give you some general notion of the
characters of mixed tints of two colours only,
and it is better in practice to confine yourself

colours, but you need not care much about permanence in
your work as yet, and they are both beautiful ; while Indigo
is marked by Field as more fugitive still, and is very ugly.
Hooker's green is a mixed colour, put in the box merely to
save you loss of time in mixing gamboge and Prussian blue.
No. 1 is the best tint of it. Violet carmine is a noble colour
for laying broken shadows with, to be worked into afterwards
with other colours.

If you wish to take up colouring seriously you had better
get Field's " Chromatography " at once ; only do not attend
to anything it says about principles or harmonies of colour ;
but only to its statements of practical serviceableness in pigments, and of their operations on each other when mixed, &c.

as much as possible to these, and to get more
complicated colours, either by putting the third
over the first blended tint, or by putting the
third into its interstices. Nothing but watchful
practice will teach you the effects that colours
have on each other when thus put over, or
beside, each other.

164. When you have got a little used to

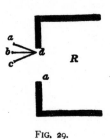

FIG. 29.

the principal combinations, place yourself at
a window which the sun does not shine in at,
commanding some simple piece of landscape:
outline this landscape roughly; then take a piece
of white cardboard, cut out a hole in it about
the size of a large pea; and supposing *R* is the
room, *a d* the window, and you are sitting at *a*,
Fig. 29, hold this cardboard a little outside of
the window, upright, and in the direction *b d*,

parallel to the side of the window, or a little turned, so as to catch more light, as at *a d*, never turned as at *c d*, or the paper will be dark. Then you will see the landscape, bit by bit, through the circular hole. Match the colours of each important bit as nearly as you can, mixing your tints with white, beside the aperture. When matched, put a touch of the same tint at the top of your paper, writing under it : " dark tree colour," " hill colour," " field colour," as the case may be. Then wash the tint away from beside the opening, and the cardboard will be ready to match another piece of the landscape.[1] When you have got the colours of the principal masses thus indicated, lay on a piece of each in your sketch in its right place, and then proceed to complete the sketch in harmony with them, by your eye.

[1] A more methodical, though under general circumstances uselessly prolix way, is to cut a square hole, some half an inch wide, in the sheet of cardboard, and a series of small circular holes in a slip of cardboard an inch wide. Pass the slip over the square opening, and match each colour beside one of the circular openings. You will thus have no occasion to wash any of the colours away. But the first rough method is generally all you want, as, after a little practice, you only need to *look* at the hue through the opening in order to be able to transfer it to your drawing at once.

165. In the course of your early experiments, you will be much struck by two things : the first, the inimitable brilliancy of light in sky and in sun-lighted things ; and the second, that among the tints which you can imitate, those which you thought the darkest will continually turn out to be in reality the lightest. Darkness of objects is estimated by us, under ordinary circumstances, much more by knowledge than by sight ; thus, a cedar or Scotch fir, at 200 yards off, will be thought of darker green than an elm or oak near us ; because we know by experience that the peculiar colour they exhibit, at that distance, is the *sign* of darkness of foliage. But when we try them through the cardboard, the near oak will be found, indeed, rather dark green, and the distant cedar, perhaps, pale grey-purple. The quantity of purple and grey in Nature is, by the way, another somewhat surprising subject of discovery.

166. Well, having ascertained thus your principal tints, you may proceed to fill up your sketch ; in doing which observe these following particulars :

(1.) Many portions of your subject appeared through the aperture in the paper brighter than the paper, as sky, sun-lighted grass, &c. Leave these portions, for the present, white; and proceed with the parts of which you can match the tints.

(2.) As you tried your subject with the cardboard, you must have observed how many changes of hue took place over small spaces. In filling up your work, try to educate your eye to perceive these differences of hue without the help of the cardboard, and lay them deliberately, like a mosaic-worker, as separate colours, preparing each carefully on your palette, and laying it as if it were a patch of coloured cloth, cut out, to be fitted neatly by its edge to the next patch; so that the *fault* of your work may be, not a slurred or misty look, but a patched bed-cover look, as if it had all been cut out with scissors. For instance, in drawing the trunk of a birch tree, there will be probably white high lights, then a pale rosy grey round them on the light side, then a (probably greenish) deeper grey on the dark side, varied by reflected colours, and, over all, rich black strips of bark and brown spots of moss. Lay first the rosy grey, leaving white for the high lights *and*

o

for the spots of moss, and not touching the dark
side. Then lay the grey for the dark side,
fitting it well up to the rosy grey of the light,
leaving also in this darker grey the white
paper in the places for the black and brown
moss; then prepare the moss colours separately for each spot, and lay each in the
white place left for it. Not one grain of
white, except that purposely left for the high
lights, must be visible when the work is done,
even through a magnifying-glass, so cunningly
must you fit the edges to each other. Finally,
take your background colours, and put them
on each side of the tree trunk, fitting them
carefully to its edge.

167. Fine work you would make of this,
wouldn't you, if you had not learned to draw
first, and could not now draw a good outline
for the stem, much less terminate a colour
mass in the outline you wanted?

Your work will look very odd for some time,
when you first begin to paint in this way,
and before you can modify it, as I shall tell
you presently how; but never mind; it is
of the greatest possible importance that you
should practise this separate laying on of

the hues, for all good colouring finally depends on it. It is, indeed, often necessary, and sometimes desirable, to lay one colour and form boldly over another: thus, in laying leaves on blue sky, it is impossible always in large pictures, or when pressed for time, to fill in the blue through the interstices of the leaves; and the great Venetians constantly lay their blue ground first, and then, having let it dry, strike the golden brown over it in the form of the leaf, leaving the under blue to shine through the gold, and subdue it to the olive-green they want. But in the most precious and perfect work each leaf is inlaid, and the blue worked round it; and, whether you use one or other mode of getting your result, it is equally necessary to be absolute and decisive in your laying the colour. Either your ground must be laid firmly first, and then your upper colour struck upon it in perfect form, for ever, thenceforward, unalterable; or else the two colours must be individually put in their places, and led up to each other till they meet at their appointed border, equally, thenceforward, unchangeable. Either process, you see, involves absolute decision.   If you once begin to slur, or change, or sketch, or try this way and that with your colour, it is all over with it and with you.   You will continually see bad copyists trying to imitate the Venetians, by daubing their colours about, and retouching, and finishing, and softening: when every touch and every added hue only lead them farther into chaos.   There is a dog between two children in a Veronese in the Louvre, which gives the copyists much employment.   He has a dark ground behind him, which Veronese has painted first, and then when it was dry, or nearly so, struck the locks of the dog's white hair over it with some half-dozen curling sweeps of his brush, right at once, and for ever.   Had one line or hair of them gone wrong, it would have been wrong for ever; no retouching could have mended it.   The poor copyists daub in first some background, and then some dog's hair; then retouch the background, then the hair; work for hours at it, expecting it always to come right to-morrow—"when it is finished."   They *may* work for centuries at it, and they will never do it.   If they can

do it with Veronese's allowance of work, half
a dozen sweeps of the hand over the dark
background, well; if not, they may ask the
dog himself whether it will ever come right,
and get true answer from him—on Launce's
conditions: "If he say 'ay,' it will; if he say
'no,' it will; if he shake his tail and say
nothing, it will."

168. (3.) Whenever you lay on a mass of
colour, be sure that however large it may be, or
however small, it shall be gradated. No colour
exists in Nature under ordinary circumstances
without gradation. If you do not see this, it
is the fault of your inexperience : you will see
it in due time, if you practise enough. But
in general you may see it at once. In the
birch trunk, for instance, the rosy grey *must*
be gradated by the roundness of the stem till
it meets the shaded side ; similarly the shaded
side is gradated by reflected light. Accordingly,
whether by adding water, or white paint, or
by unequal force of touch (this you will do
at pleasure, according to the texture you wish
to produce), you must, in every tint you lay
on, make it a little paler at one part than
another, and get an even gradation between

the two depths.   This is very like laying
down a formal law or recipe for you; but
you will find it is merely the assertion of a
natural fact.   It is not indeed physically impossible to meet with an ungradated piece of
colour, but it is so supremely improbable,
that you had better get into the habit of ask-
ing yourself invariably, when you are going
to copy a tint—not "Is that gradated?" but
"Which way is that gradated?" and at least
in ninety-nine out of a hundred instances,
you will be able to answer decisively after
a careful glance, though the gradation may
have been so subtle that you did not see it
at first.   And it does not matter how small
the touch of colour may be, though not larger
than the smallest pin's head, if one part of it
is not darker than the rest, it is a bad touch;
for it is not merely because the natural fact
is so, that your colour should be gradated; the
preciousness and pleasantness of the colour itself depends more on this than on any other
of its qualities, for gradation is to colours
just what curvature is to lines, both being felt
to be beautiful by the pure instinct of every
human mind, and both, considered as types,

expressing the law of gradual change and progress in the human soul itself. What the difference is in mere beauty between a gradated
and ungradated colour, may be seen easily
by laying an even tint of rose-colour on paper,
and putting a rose leaf beside it. The vic-
torious beauty of the rose, as compared with
other flowers, depends wholly on the delicacy
and quantity of its colour gradations, all other
flowers being either less rich in gradation,
not having so many folds of leaf; or less
tender, being patched and veined instead of
flushed.

169. (4.) But observe, it is not enough
in general that colour should be gradated by
being made merely paler or darker at one
place than another. Generally colour changes
as it diminishes, and is not merely darker
at one spot, but also purer at one spot than
anywhere else. It does not in the least follow
that the darkest spot should be the purest;
still less so that the lightest should be the
purest. Very often the two gradations more
or less cross each other, one passing in one
direction from paleness to darkness, another
in another direction from purity to dulness,

but there will almost always be both of them,
however reconciled; and you must never be
satisfied with a piece of colour until you have
got both : that is to say, every piece of blue
that you lay on must be *quite* blue only at
some given spot, nor that a large spot; and
must be gradated from that into less pure
blue,—greyish blue, or greenish blue, or pur-
plish blue,—over all the rest of the space it
occupies. And this you must do in one of
three ways : either, while the colour is wet,
mix with it the colour which is to subdue it,
adding gradually a little more and a little
more; or else, when the colour is quite dry,
strike a gradated touch of another colour over
it, leaving only a point of the first tint visible ;
or else, lay the subduing tints on in small
touches, as in the exercise of tinting the
chess-board. Of each of these methods I have
something to tell you separately; but that is
distinct from the subject of gradation, which
I must not quit without once more pressing
upon you the preëminent necessity of introducing it everywhere. I have profound dislike of anything like habit of hand, and yet,
in this one instance, I feel almost tempted

to encourage you to get into a habit of never
touching paper with colour, without securing
a gradation.   You will not, in Turner's largest
oil pictures, perhaps six or seven feet long
by four or five high, find one spot of colour
as large as a grain of wheat ungradated : and
you will find in practice, that brilliancy of
hue, and vigour of light, and even the aspect
of transparency in shade, are essentially dependent on this character alone ; hardness,
coldness, and opacity resulting far more from
equality of colour than from nature of colour.
Give me some mud off a city crossing, some
ochre out of a gravel pit, a little whitening,
and some coal-dust, and I will paint you a
luminous picture, if you give me time to
gradate my mud, and subdue my dust : but
though you had the red of the ruby, the blue of
the gentian, snow for the light, and amber for
the gold, you cannot paint a luminous picture,
if you keep the masses of those colours un-
broken in purity, and unvarying in depth.

170. (5.) Next, note the three processes by
which gradation and other characters are to be
obtained :

A. Mixing while the colour is wet.

You may be confused by my first telling you
to lay on the hues in separate patches, and
then telling you to mix hues together as you
lay them on : but the separate masses are to
be laid, when colours distinctly oppose each
other at a given limit ; the hues to be mixed,
when they palpitate one through the other,
or fade one into the other.   It is better to err
a little on the distinct side.   Thus I told you
to paint the dark and light sides of the birch
trunk separately, though, in reality, the two
tints change, as the trunk turns away from the
light, gradually one into the other ; and, after
being laid separately on, will need some farther
touching to harmonise them : but they do so
in a very narrow space, marked distinctly all
the way up the trunk, and it is easier and
safer, therefore, to keep them separate at first.
Whereas it often happens that the whole beauty
of two colours will depend on the one being
continued well through the other, and playing
in the midst of it : blue and green often do
so in water ; blue and grey, or purple and
scarlet, in sky : in hundreds of such instances
the most beautiful and truthful results may be
obtained by laying one colour into the other

while wet ; judging wisely how far it will spread,
or blending it with the brush in somewhat
thicker consistence of wet body-colour; only
observe, never mix in this way two *mixtures;*
let the colour you lay into the other be always
a simple, not a compound tint.

171. B. Laying one colour over another.

If you lay on a solid touch of vermilion,
and after it is quite dry, strike a little very wet
carmine quickly over it, you will obtain a much
more brilliant red than by mixing the carmine
and vermilion. Similarly, if you lay a dark
colour first, and strike a little blue or white
body-colour lightly over it, you will get a more
beautiful grey than by mixing the colour and
the blue or white. In very perfect painting,
artifices of this kind are continually used ; but
I would not have you trust much to them :
they are apt to make you think too much of
quality of colour. I should like you to depend
on little more than the dead colours, simply
laid on, only observe always this, that the *less*
colour you do the work with, the better it will
always be :[1] so that if you had laid a red

[1] If colours were twenty times as costly as they are, we
should have many more good painters. If I were Chancellor

colour, and you want a purple one above, do not mix the purple on your palette and lay it on so thick as to overpower the red, but take a little thin blue from your palette, and lay it lightly over the red, so as to let the red be seen through, and thus produce the required purple; and if you want a green hue over a blue one, do not lay a quantity of green on the blue, but a *little* yellow, and so on, always bringing the under colour into service as far as you possibly can.   If, however, the colour beneath is wholly opposed to the one you have to lay on, as, suppose, if green is to be laid over scarlet, you must either remove the required parts of the under colour daintily first with your knife, or with water; or else, lay solid white over it massively, and leave that to dry, and then glaze the white with the upper colour. This is better, in general, than laying the upper colour itself so thick as to conquer the ground, which, in fact, if it be a transparent colour,

of the Exchequer I would lay a tax of twenty shillings a cake on all colours except black, Prussian blue, Vandyke brown, and Chinese white, which I would leave for students. I don't say this jestingly; I believe such a tax would do more to advance real art than a great many schools of design.

you cannot do.   Thus, if you have to strike warm boughs and leaves of trees over blue sky, and they are too intricate to have their places left for them in laying the blue, it is better to lay them first in solid white, and then glaze with sienna and ochre, than to mix the sienna and white; though, of course, the process is longer and more troublesome.   Nevertheless, if the forms of touches required are very delicate, the after glazing is impossible. You must then mix the warm colour thick at once, and so use it : and this is often necessary for delicate grasses, and such other fine threads of light in foreground work.

172. C. Breaking one colour in small points through or over another.

This is the most important of all processes in good modern[1] oil and water-colour painting, but you need not hope to attain very great skill in it.   To do it well is very laborious, and requires such skill and delicacy of hand as can only be acquired by unceasing practice.

---

[1] I say *modern*, because Titian's quiet way of blending colours, which is the perfectly right one, is not understood now by any artist. The best colour we reach is got by stippling ; but this is not quite right.

But you will find advantage in noting the following points :

173. (*a.*) In distant effects of rich subject, wood, or rippled water, or broken clouds, much may be done by touches or crumbling dashes of rather dry colour, with other colours afterwards put cunningly into the interstices. The more you practise this, when the subject evidently calls for it, the more your eye will enjoy the higher qualities of colour. The process is, in fact, the carrying out of the principle of separate colours to the utmost possible refinement; using atoms of colour in juxtaposition, instead of large spaces. And note, in filling up minute interstices of this kind, that if you want the colour you fill them with to show brightly, it is better to put a rather positive point of it, with a little white left beside or round it in the interstice, than to put a pale tint of the colour over the whole interstice. Yellow or orange will hardly show, if pale, in small spaces; but they show brightly in firm touches, however small, with white beside them.

174. (*b.*) If a colour is to be darkened by superimposed portions of another, it is, in many cases,

better to lay the uppermost colour in rather
vigorous small touches, like finely chopped
straw, over the under one, than to lay it on
as a tint, for two reasons: the first, that the
play of the two colours together is pleasant to
the eye; the second, that much expression of
form may be got by wise administration of the
upper dark touches. In distant mountains they
may be made pines of, or broken crags, or
villages, or stones, or whatever you choose;
in clouds they may indicate the direction of the
rain, the roll and outline of the cloud masses;
and in water, the minor waves. All noble
effects of dark atmosphere are got in good
water-colour drawing by these two expedients,
interlacing the colours, or retouching the lower
one with fine darker drawing in an upper.
Sponging and washing for dark atmospheric
effect is barbarous, and mere tyro's work,
though it is often useful for passages of delicate atmospheric light.

175. (c.) When you have time, practise
the production of mixed tints by interlaced
touches of the pure colours out of which
they are formed, and use the process at the
parts of your sketches where you wish to get

rich and luscious effects.   Study the works of William Hunt, of the Old Water-colour Society, in this respect, continually, and make frequent memoranda of the variegations in flowers; not painting the flower completely, but laying the ground colour of one petal, and painting the spots on it with studious precision: a series of single petals of lilies, geraniums, tulips, &c., numbered with proper reference to their position in the flower, will be interesting to you on many grounds besides those of art.   Be careful to get the gradated distribution of the spots well followed in the calceolarias, foxgloves, and the like; and work out the odd, indefinite hues of the spots themselves with minute grains of pure interlaced colour, otherwise you will never get their richness or bloom.   You will be surprised to find as you do this, first, the universality of the law of gradation we have so much insisted upon; secondly, that Nature is just as economical of *her* fine colours as I have told you to be of yours.   You would think, by the way she paints, that her colours cost her something enormous; she will only give you a single pure touch, just where the

petal turns into light ; but down in the bell all
is subdued, and under the petal all is subdued,
even in the showiest flower. What you
thought was bright blue is, when you look
close, only dusty grey, or green, or purple,
or every colour in the world at once, only a
single gleam or streak of pure blue in the
centre of it. And so with all her colours.
Sometimes I have really thought her miserli-
ness intolerable : in a gentian, for instance,
the way she economises her ultramarine down
in the bell is a little too bad.[1]

176. Next, respecting general tone. I said,
just now, that, for the sake of students, my
tax should not be laid on black or on white
pigments ; but if you mean to be a colourist,
you must lay a tax on them yourself when
you begin to use true colour; that is to say,
you must use them little, and make of them
much. There is no better test of your colour
tones being good, than your having made the
white in your picture precious, and the black
conspicuous.

177. I say, first, the white precious. I do
not mean merely glittering or brilliant: it is

[1] See Note 6 in Appendix I.

P

easy to scratch white sea-gulls out of black
clouds, and dot clumsy foliage with chalky
dew; but when white is well managed, it
ought to be strangely delicious,—tender as
well as bright,—like inlaid mother of pearl, or
white roses washed in milk. The eye ought
to seek it for rest, brilliant though it may be;
and to feel it as a space of strange, heavenly
paleness in the midst of the flushing of the
colours. This effect you can only reach by
general depth of middle tint, by absolutely
refusing to allow any white to exist except
where you need it, and by keeping the white
itself subdued by grey, except at a few points
of chief lustre.

178. Secondly, you must make the black
conspicuous. However small a point of black
may be, it ought to catch the eye, otherwise
your work is too heavy in the shadow. All
the ordinary shadows should be of some *colour*,
—never black, nor approaching black, they
should be evidently and always of a luminous
nature, and the black should look strange
among them; never occurring except in a
black object, or in small points indicative of
intense shade in the very centre of masses

of shadow. Shadows of absolutely negative grey, however, may be beautifully used with white, or with gold; but still though the black thus, in subdued strength, becomes spacious, it should always be conspicuous; the spectator should notice this grey neutrality with some wonder, and enjoy, all the more intensely on account of it, the gold colour and the white which it relieves. Of all the great colourists Velasquez is the greatest master of the black chords. His black is more precious than most other people's crimson.

179. It is not, however, only white and black which you must make valuable; you must give rare worth to every colour you use; but the white and black ought to separate themselves quaintly from the rest, while the other colours should be continually passing one into the other, being all evidently companions in the same gay world; while the white, black, and neutral grey should stand monkishly aloof in the midst of them. You may melt your crimson into purple, your purple into blue, and your blue into green, but you must not melt any of them into black. You should, however, try, as I said,

to give preciousness to all your colours ; and
this especially by never using a grain more
than will just do the work, and giving each
hue the highest value by opposition. All fine
colouring, like fine drawing, is delicate ; and
so delicate that if, at last, you *see* the colour
you are putting on, you are putting on too
much. You ought to feel a change wrought
in the general tone, by touches of colour
which individually are too pale to be seen ;
and if there is one atom of any colour in the
whole picture which is unnecessary to it, that
atom hurts it.

180. Notice also that nearly all good compound colours are *odd* colours. You shall
look at a hue in a good painter's work ten
minutes before you know what to call it.
You thought it was brown, presently you feel
that it is red ; next that there is, somehow,
yellow in it ; presently afterwards that there
is blue in it. If you try to copy it you will
always find your colour too warm or too cold
—no colour in the box will seem to have an
affinity with it ; and yet it will be as pure as
if it were laid at a single touch with a single
colour.

181. As to the choice and harmony of
colours in general, if you cannot choose and
harmonise them by instinct, you will never
do it at all.   If you need examples of utterly
harsh and horrible colour, you may find plenty
given in treatises upon colouring, to illustrate
the laws of harmony; and if you want to
colour beautifully, colour as best pleases yourself at *quiet times*, not so as to catch the eye,
nor look as if it were clever or difficult to
colour in that way, but so that the colour
may be pleasant to you when you are happy
or thoughtful.   Look much at the morning
and evening sky, and much at simple flowers
—dog-roses, wood-hyacinths, violets, poppies,
thistles, heather, and such like,—as Nature
arranges them in the woods and fields.   If
ever any scientific person tells you that two
colours are " discordant," make a note of the
two colours, and put them together whenever
you can.   I have actually heard people say
that blue and green were discordant; the
two colours which Nature seems to intend
never to be separated, and never to be felt,
either of them, in its full beauty without the
other!—a peacock's neck, or a blue sky

through green leaves, or a blue wave with green lights through it, being precisely the loveliest things, next to clouds at sunrise, in this coloured world of ours. If you have a good eye for colours, you will soon find out how constantly Nature puts purple and green together, purple and scarlet, green and blue, yellow and neutral grey, and the like ; and how she strikes these colour-concords for general tones, and then works into them with innumerable subordinate ones; and you will gradually come to like what she does, and find out new and beautiful chords of colour in her work every day. If you enjoy them, depend upon it you will paint them to a certain point right : or, at least, if you do not enjoy them, you are certain to paint them wrong. If colour does not give you intense pleasure, let it alone; depend upon it, you are only tormenting the eyes and senses of people who feel colour, whenever you touch it ; and that is unkind and improper.

182. You will find, also, your power of colouring depend much on your state of health and right balance of mind ; when you are

fatigued or ill you will not see colours well,
and when you are ill-tempered you will not
choose them well: thus, though not infallibly
a test of character in individuals, colour power
is a great sign of mental health in nations;
when they are in a state of intellectual decline,
their colouring always gets dull.[1]   You must
also take great care not to be misled by
affected talk about colours from people who
have not the gift of it: numbers are eager
and voluble about it who probably never in
all their lives received one genuine colour-
sensation.   The modern religionists of the
school of Overbeck are just like people who
eat slate-pencil and chalk, and assure everybody that they are nicer and purer than straw-
berries and plums.

183. Take care also never to be misled
into any idea that colour can help or display
form; colour[2] always disguises form, and is
meant to do so.

[1] The worst general character that colour can possibly
have is a prevalent tendency to a dirty yellowish green, like
that of a decaying heap of vegetables ; this colour is *accurately*
indicative of decline or paralysis in missal-painting.

[2] That is to say, local colour inherent in the object.   The
gradations of colour in the various shadows belonging to

184. It is a favourite dogma among modern writers on colour that "warm colours" (reds and yellows) "approach," or express nearness, and "cold colours" (blue and grey) "retire," or express distance.   So far is this from being the case, that no expression of distance in the world is so great as that of the gold and orange in twilight sky.   Colours, as such, are ABSOLUTELY inexpressive respecting distance.   It is their quality (as depth, delicacy, &c.) which expresses distance, not their tint. A blue bandbox set on the same shelf with a yellow one will not look an inch farther off, but a red or orange cloud, in the upper sky, will always appear to be beyond a blue cloud

various lights exhibit form, and therefore no one but a colourist can ever draw *forms* perfectly (see Modern Painters, vol. iv. chap. iii. at the end) ; but all notions of explaining form by superimposed colour, as in architectural mouldings, are absurd.   Colour adorns form, but does not interpret it.   An apple is prettier because it is striped, but it does not look a bit rounder ; and a cheek is prettier because it is flushed, but you would see the form of the cheek bone better if it were not.   Colour may, indeed, detach one shape from another, as in grounding a bas-relief, but it always diminishes the appearance of projection, and whether you put blue, purple, red, yellow, or green, for your ground, the bas-relief will be just as clearly or just as imperfectly relieved, as long as the colours are of equal depth.   The blue ground will not retire the hundredth part of an inch more than the red one.

close to us, as it is in reality.   It is quite true
that in certain objects, blue is a *sign* of distance; but that is not because blue is a retiring colour, but because the mist in the air
is blue, and therefore any warm colour which
has not strength of light enough to pierce
the mist is lost or subdued in its blue: but
blue is no more, on this account, a "retiring colour," than brown is a retiring colour,
because, when stones are seen through brown
water, the deeper they lie the browner they
look; or than yellow is a retiring colour,
because, when objects are seen through a
London fog, the farther off they are the
yellower they look.   Neither blue, nor yellow,
nor red, can have, as such, the smallest power
of expressing either nearness or distance: they
express them only under the peculiar circumstances which render them at the moment, or
in that place, *signs* of nearness or distance.
Thus, vivid orange in an orange is a sign of
nearness, for if you put the orange a great
way off, its colour will not look so bright;
but vivid orange in sky is a sign of distance,
because you cannot get the colour of orange
in a cloud near you.   So purple in a violet

or a hyacinth is a sign of nearness, because
the closer you look at them the more purple
you see.   But purple in a mountain is a sign
of distance, because a mountain close to you
is not purple, but green or grey.   It may,
indeed, be generally assumed that a tender
or pale colour will more or less express distance, and a powerful or dark colour nearness;
but even this is not always so.   Heathery
hills will usually give a pale and tender purple
near, and an intense and dark purple far
away; the rose colour of sunset on snow is
pale on the snow at your feet, deep and full
on the snow in the distance; and the green
of a Swiss lake is pale in the clear waves on
the beach, but intense as an emerald in the
sunstreak six miles from shore.   And in any
case, when the foreground is in strong light,
with much water about it, or white surface,
casting intense reflections, all its colours may
be perfectly delicate, pale, and faint; while the
distance, when it is in shadow, may relieve
the whole foreground with intense darks of
purple, blue green, or ultramarine blue.   So
that, on the whole, it is quite hopeless and
absurd to expect any help from laws of " aërial

perspective." Look for the natural effects, and set them down as fully as you can, and as faithfully, and *never* alter a colour because it won't look in its right place. Put the colour strong, if it be strong, though far off; faint, if it be faint, though close to you. Why should you suppose that Nature always means you to know exactly how far one thing is from another? She certainly intends you always to enjoy her colouring, but she does not wish you always to measure her space. You would be hard put to it, every time you painted the sun setting, if you had to express his 95,000,000 miles of distance in "aërial perspective."

185. There is, however, I think, one law about distance, which has some claims to be considered a constant one : namely, that dullness and heaviness of colour are more or less indicative of nearness. All distant colour is *pure* colour: it may not be bright, but it is clear and lovely, not opaque nor soiled ; for the air and light coming between us and any earthy or imperfect colour, purify or harmonise it ; hence a bad colourist is peculiarly incapable of expressing distance. I do not of course mean that you are to use bad colours

in your foreground by way of making it come forward; but only that a failure in colour, there, will not put it out of its place; while a failure in colour in the distance will at once do away with its remoteness; your dull-coloured foreground will still be a foreground, though ill-painted; but your ill-painted distance will not be merely a dull distance,—it will be no distance at all.

186. I have only one thing more to advise you, namely, never to colour petulantly or hurriedly. You will not, indeed, be able, if you attend properly to your colouring, to get anything like the quantity of form you could in a chiaroscuro sketch; nevertheless, if you do not dash or rush at your work, nor do it lazily, you may always get enough form to be satisfactory. An extra quarter of an hour, distributed in quietness over the course of the whole study, may just make the difference between a quite intelligible drawing, and a slovenly and obscure one. If you determine well beforehand what outline each piece of colour is to have, and, when it is on the paper, guide it without nervousness, as far as you can, into the form required; and then, after it

is dry, consider thoroughly what touches are needed to complete it, before laying one of them on ; you will be surprised to find how masterly the work will soon look, as compared with a hurried or ill-considered sketch. In no process that I know of—least of all in sketching—can time be really gained by precipitation. It is gained only by caution ; and

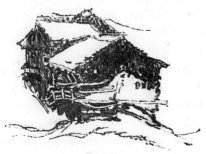

FIG. 30.

gained in all sorts of ways ; for not only truth of form, but force of light, is always added by an intelligent and shapely laying of the shadow colours. You may often make a simple flat tint, rightly gradated and edged, express a complicated piece of subject without a single retouch. The two Swiss cottages, for instance, with their balconies, and glittering

windows, and general character of shingly
eaves, are expressed in Fig. 30 with one tint
of grey, and a few dispersed spots and lines
of it ; all of which you ought to be able to lay
on without more than thrice dipping your
brush, and without a single touch after the
tint is dry.

187. Here, then, for I cannot without
coloured illustrations tell you more, I must
leave you to follow out the subject for yourself, with such help as you may receive from
the water-colour drawings accessible to you ;
or from any of the little treatises on their art
which have been published lately by our
water-colour painters.[1]   But do not trust
much to works of this kind.   You may get
valuable hints from them as to mixture of
colours ; and here and there you will find a
useful artifice or process explained ; but
nearly all such books are written only to
help idle amateurs to a meretricious skill, and
they are full of precepts and principles which
may, for the most part, be interpreted by their

---

[1] See, however, at the close of this letter, the notice of
one more point connected with the management of colour,
under the head " Law of Harmony."

precise negatives, and then acted upon with
advantage. Most of them praise boldness,
when the only safe attendant spirit of a beginner is caution ;—advise velocity, when the
first condition of success is deliberation ;—and
plead for generalisation, when all the founda-
tions of power must be laid in knowledge of
speciality.

188. And now, in the last place, I have
a few things to tell you respecting that
dangerous nobleness of consummate art,—
COMPOSITION. For though it is quite unnecessary for you yet awhile to attempt it,
and it *may* be inexpedient for you to attempt
it at all, you ought to know what it means,
and to look for and enjoy it in the art of
others.

Composition means, literally and simply,
putting several things together, so as to make
one thing out of them ; the nature and goodness of which they all have a share in producing. Thus a musician composes an air,
by putting notes together in certain relations ;
a poet composes a poem, by putting thoughts
and words in pleasant order ; and a painter a

picture, by putting thoughts, forms, and colours
in pleasant order.

In all these cases, observe, an intended
unity must be the result of composition. A
paviour cannot be said to compose the heap
of stones which he empties from his cart, nor
the sower the handful of seed which he
scatters from his hand. It is the essence of
composition that everything should be in a
determined place, perform an intended part,
and act, in that part, advantageously for
everything that is connected with it.

189. Composition, understood in this pure
sense, is the type, in the arts of mankind, of
the Providential government of the world.[1]   It
is an exhibition, in the order given to notes,
or colours, or forms, of the advantage of perfect fellowship, discipline, and contentment.
In a well-composed air, no note, however
short or low, can be spared, but the least is
as necessary as the greatest: no note, however prolonged, is tedious; but the others prepare for, and are benefited by, its duration: no
note, however high, is tyrannous; the others

---

[1] See farther, on this subject, Modern Painters, vol. iv.
chap. viii. § 6.

prepare for, and are benefited by, its exalta-
tion : no note, however low, is overpowered ;
the others prepare for, and sympathise with,
its humility : and the result is, that each and
every note has a value in the position assigned
to it, which, by itself, it never possessed, and
of which, by separation from the others, it
would instantly be deprived.

190. Similarly, in a good poem, each word
and thought enhances the value of those which
precede and follow it; and every syllable has
a loveliness which depends not so much on its
abstract sound as on its position.   Look at
the same word in a dictionary, and you will
hardly recognise it.

Much more in a great picture ; every line
and colour is so arranged as to advantage the
rest.   None are inessential, however slight ;
and none are independent, however forcible.
It is not enough that they truly represent
natural objects ; but they must fit into certain
places, and gather into certain harmonious
groups : so that, for instance, the red chimney
of a cottage is not merely set in its place as a
chimney, but that it may affect, in a certain
way pleasurable to the eye, the pieces of

Q

green or blue in other parts of the picture;
and we ought to see that the work is masterly,
merely by the positions and quantities of these
patches of green, red, and blue, even at a distance which renders it perfectly impossible to
determine what the colours represent : or to
see whether the red is a chimney, or an old
woman's cloak; and whether the blue is
smoke, sky, or water.

191. It seems to be appointed, in order to
remind us, in all we do, of the great laws
of Divine government and human polity, that
composition in the arts should strongly affect
every order of mind, however unlearned or
thoughtless.   Hence the popular delight in
rhythm and metre, and in simple musical
melodies.   But it is also appointed that *power*
of composition in the fine arts should be an
exclusive attribute of great intellect.   All men
can more or less copy what they see, and, more
or less, remember it : powers of reflection and
investigation are also common to us all, so that
the decision of inferiority in these rests only on
questions of *degree*.   A. has a better memory
than B., and C. reflects more profoundly than D.
But the gift of composition is not given *at all*

to more than one man in a thousand ; in its highest range, it does not occur above three or four times in a century.

192. It follows, from these general truths, that it is impossible to give rules which will enable you to compose. You might much more easily receive rules to enable you to be witty. If it were possible to be witty by rule, wit would cease to be either admirable or amusing : if it were possible to compose melody by rule, Mozart and Cimarosa need not have been born : if it were possible to compose pictures by rule, Titian and Veronese would be ordinary men. The essence of composition lies precisely in the fact of its being unteachable, in its being the operation of an individual mind of range and power exalted above others.

But though no one can *invent* by rule, there are some simple laws of arrangement which it is well for you to know, because, though they will not enable you to produce a good picture, they will often assist you to set forth what goodness may be in your work in a more telling way than you could have done otherwise ; and by tracing them in the work of good

composers, you may better understand the grasp
of their imagination, and the power it possesses
over their materials. I shall briefly state the
chief of these laws.

I. THE LAW OF PRINCIPALITY.

193. The great object of composition being
always to secure unity; that is, to make out
of many things one whole; the first mode in
which this can be effected is, by determining

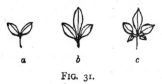

a   b   c

FIG. 31.

that *one* feature shall be more important than
all the rest, and that the others shall group
with it in subordinate positions.

This is the simplest law of ordinary ornamentation. Thus the group of two leaves,
a, Fig. 31, is unsatisfactory, because it has no
leading leaf; but that at *b is* prettier, because
it has a head or master leaf; and *c* more satisfactory still, because the subordination of the
other members to this head leaf is made more

manifest by their gradual loss of size as they fall back from it.   Hence part of the pleasure we have in the Greek honeysuckle ornament, and such others.

194. Thus, also, good pictures have always one light larger and brighter than the other lights, or one figure more prominent than the other figures, or one mass of colour dominant over all the other masses ; and in general you will find it much benefit your sketch if you manage that there shall be one light on the cottage wall, or one blue cloud in the sky, which may attract the eye as leading light, or leading gloom, above all others.   But the observance of the rule is often so cunningly concealed by the great composers, that its force is hardly at first traceable ; and you will generally find they are vulgar pictures in which the law is strikingly manifest.

195. This may be simply illustrated by musical melody : for instance, in such phrases as this—

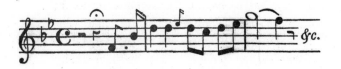

one note (here the upper G) rules the whole
passage, and has the full energy of it concentrated in itself. 'Such passages, corresponding to completely subordinated compositions
in painting, are apt to be wearisome if often
repeated. But, in such a phrase as this—

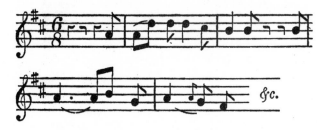

it is very difficult to say which is the principal note. The A in the last bar is slightly
dominant, but there is a very equal current
of power running through the whole; and
such passages rarely weary. And this principle holds through vast scales of arrangement; so that in the grandest compositions,
such as Paul Veronese's Marriage in Cana,
or Raphael's Disputa, it is not easy to fix
at once on the principal figure; and very
commonly the figure which is really chief
does not catch the eye at first, but is gradually

felt to be more and more conspicuous as we gaze. Thus in Titian's grand composition of the Cornaro Family, the figure meant to be principal is a youth of fifteen or sixteen, whose portrait it was evidently the painter's object to make as interesting as possible. But a grand Madonna, and a St. George with a drifting banner, and many figures more, occupy the centre of the picture, and first catch the eye; little by little we are led away from them to a gleam of pearly light in the lower corner, and find that, from the head which it shines upon, we can turn our eyes no more.

196. As, in every good picture, nearly all laws of design are more or less exemplified, it will, on the whole, be an easier way of explaining them to analyse one composition thoroughly, than to give instances from various works. I shall therefore take one of Turner's simplest; which will allow us, so to speak, easily to decompose it, and illustrate each law by it as we proceed.

Fig. 32 is a rude sketch of the arrangement of the whole subject; the old bridge over the Moselle at Coblentz, the town of Coblentz on the right, Ehrenbreitstein on the left. The leading or master feature is, of course, the tower on the bridge. It is kept from being *too* principal by an important group on each side of it; the boats, on the right, and Ehrenbreitstein beyond. The boats are large in

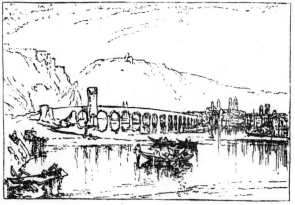

FIG. 32.

mass, and more forcible in colour, but they are broken into small divisions, while the tower is simple, and therefore it still leads. Ehrenbreitstein is noble in its mass, but so reduced by aërial perspective of colour that it cannot contend with the tower, which therefore holds the eye, and becomes the key of

the picture.   We shall see presently how
the very objects which seem at first to contend with it for the mastery are made, occultly,
to increase its preëminence.

2. THE LAW OF REPETITION.

197. Another important means of expressing unity is to mark some kind of sympathy
among the different objects, and perhaps the
pleasantest, because most surprising, kind of
sympathy, is when one group imitates or re-
peats another; not in the way of balance or
symmetry, but subordinately, like a far-away
and broken echo of it. Prout has insisted
much on this law in all his writings on composition; and I think it is even more authori-
tatively present in the minds of most great
composers than the law of principality.[1]   It
is quite curious to see the pains that Turner
sometimes takes to echo an important passage
of colour; in the Pembroke Castle for instance,
there are two fishing-boats, one with a red,
and another with a white sail. In a line with
them, on the beach, are two fish in precisely

[1] See Note 7 in Appendix I.

the same relative positions; one red and one white.   It is observable that he uses the artifice chiefly in pictures where he wishes to obtain an expression of repose : in my notice of the plate of Scarborough, in the series of the Harbours of England, I have already had occasion to dwell on this point ; and I extract in the note [1] one or two sentences which explain the principle.   In the composition I have chosen for our illustration, this reduplication is employed to a singular extent. The tower, or leading feature, is first repeated by the low echo of it to the left ; put your finger over this lower tower, and see how the picture is spoiled.   Then the spires of Coblentz are all arranged in couples (how they are arranged in reality does not matter ; when we are composing a great picture, we must

[1] " In general, throughout Nature, reflection and repetition are peaceful things, associated with the idea of quiet succession in events ; that one day should be like another day, or one history the repetition of another history, being more or less results of quietness, while dissimilarity and non-succession are results of interference and disquietude.   Thus, though an echo actually increases the quantity of sound heard, its repetition of the note or syllable gives an idea of calmness attainable in no other way ; hence also the feeling of calm given to a landscape by the voice of a cuckoo."

play the towers about till they come right, as
fearlessly as if they were chessmen instead
of cathedrals). The dual arrangement of
these towers would have been too easily
seen, were it not for the little one which pretends to make a triad of the last group on
the right, but is so faint as hardly to be discernible : it just takes off the attention from
the artifice, helped in doing so by the mast
at the head of the boat, which, however, has
instantly its own duplicate put at the stern.[1]
Then there is the large boat near, and its echo
beyond it. That echo is divided into two
again, and each of those two smaller boats
has two figures in it ; while two figures are
also sitting together on the great rudder
that lies half in the water, and half aground.
Then, finally, the great mass of Ehrenbreitstein, which appears at first to have no answering form, has almost its *facsimile* in the
bank on which the girl is sitting ; this bank
is as absolutely essential to the completion

[1] This is obscure in the rude woodcut, the masts being so
delicate that they are confused among the lines of reflection.
In the original they have orange light upon them, relieved
against purple behind.

of the picture as any object in the whole series. All this is done to deepen the effect of repose.

198. Symmetry, or the balance of parts or masses in nearly equal opposition, is one of the conditions of treatment under the law of Repetition. For the opposition, in a sym-metrical object, is of like things reflecting each other: it is not the balance of contrary natures (like that of day and night), but of like natures or like forms; one side of a leaf being set like the reflection of the other in water.

Symmetry in Nature is, however, never formal nor accurate. She takes the greatest care to secure some difference between the corresponding things or parts of things; and an approximation to accurate symmetry is only permitted in animals, because their motions secure perpetual difference between the balancing parts. Stand before a mirror; hold your arms in precisely the same position at each side, your head upright, your body straight; divide your hair exactly in the middle and get it as nearly as you can into exactly the same shape over each ear; and

you will see the effect of accurate symmetry :
you will see, no less, how all grace and power
in the human form result from the interference of motion and life with symmetry, and
from the reconciliation of its balance with its
changefulness. Your position, as seen in the
mirror, is the highest type of symmetry as
understood by modern architects.

199. In many sacred compositions, living
symmetry, the balance of harmonious oppo-
sites, is one of the profoundest sources of
their power : almost any works of the early
painters, Angelico, Perugino, Giotto, &c., will
furnish you with notable instances of it. The
Madonna of Perugino in the National Gallery,
with the angel Michael on one side and
Raphael on the other, is as beautiful an example as you can have.

In landscape, the principle of balance is
more or less carried out, in proportion to the
wish of the painter to express disciplined
calmness. In bad compositions, as in bad
architecture, it is formal, a tree on one side
answering a tree on the other; but in good
compositions, as in graceful statues, it is
always easy and sometimes hardly traceable.

In the Coblentz, however, you cannot have
much difficulty in seeing how the boats on
one side of the tower and the figures on the
other are set in nearly equal balance; the
tower, as a central mass, uniting both.

3. THE LAW OF CONTINUITY.

200. Another important and pleasurable
way of expressing unity, is by giving some
orderly succession to a number of objects
more or less similar. And this succession
is most interesting when it is connected
with some gradual change in the aspect or
character of the objects. Thus the succession of the pillars of a cathedral aisle is
most interesting when they retire in perspective, becoming more and more obscure in
distance: so the succession of mountain pro-
montories one behind another, on the flanks
of a valley; so the succession of clouds, fad-
ing farther and farther towards the horizon;
each promontory and each cloud being of
different shape, yet all evidently following in
a calm and appointed order. If there be no
change at all in the shape or size of the

objects, there is no continuity; there is only
repetition — monotony. It is the change in
shape which suggests the idea of their being
individually free, and able to escape, if they

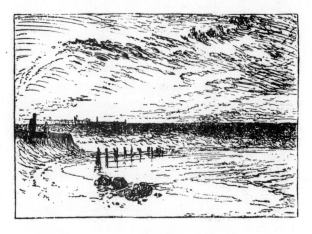

FIG. 33.

liked, from the law that rules them, and yet
submitting to it.

201. I will leave our chosen illustrative
composition for a moment to take up another,
still more expressive of this law. It is one
of Turner's most tender studies, a sketch on
Calais Sands at sunset; so delicate in the

expression of wave and cloud, that it is of
no use for me to try to reach it with any
kind of outline in a woodcut; but the rough
sketch, Fig. 33, is enough to give an idea of
its arrangement. The aim of the painter has
been to give the intensest expression of repose,
together with the enchanted, lulling, monotonous motion of cloud and wave. All the
clouds are moving in innumerable ranks after
the sun, meeting towards that point in the
horizon where he has set; and the tidal
waves gain in winding currents upon the
sand, with that stealthy haste in which they
cross each other so quietly, at their edges;
just folding one over another as they meet, like
a little piece of ruffled silk, and leaping up a
little as two children kiss and clap their hands,
and then going on again, each in its silent
hurry, drawing pointed arches on the sand
as their thin edges intersect in parting. But
all this would not have been enough expressed
without the line of the old pier-timbers, black
with weeds, strained and bent by the storm
waves, and now seeming to stoop in following
one another, like dark ghosts escaping slowly
from the cruelty of the pursuing sea.

202. I need not, I hope, point out to the reader the illustration of this law of continuance in the subject chosen for our general illustration. It was simply that gradual succession of the retiring arches of the bridge which induced Turner to paint the subject at all; and it was this same principle which led him always to seize on subjects including long bridges wherever he could find them ; but especially, observe, unequal bridges, having the highest arch at one side rather than at the centre. There is a reason for this, irrespective of general laws of composition, and connected with the nature of rivers, which I may as well stop a minute to tell you about, and let you rest from the study of composition.

203. All rivers, small or large, agree in one character, they like to lean a little on one side : they cannot bear to have their channels deepest in the middle, but will always, if they can, have one bank to sun themselves upon, and another to get cool under ; one shingly shore to play over, where they may be shallow, and foolish, and childlike, and another steep shore, under which they can pause, and purify themselves, and get their strength of

R

waves fully together for due occasion. Rivers in this way are just like wise men, who keep one side of their life for play, and another for work; and can be brilliant, and chattering, and transparent, when they are at ease, and yet take deep counsel on the other side when they set themselves to their main purpose. And rivers are just in this divided, also, like wicked and good men: the good rivers have serviceable deep places all along their banks, that ships can sail in; but the wicked rivers go scooping irregularly under their banks until they get full of strangling eddies, which no boat can row over without being twisted against the rocks; and pools like wells, which no one can get out of but the water-kelpie that lives at the bottom; but, wicked or good, the rivers all agree in having two kinds of sides. Now the natural way in which a village stone-mason therefore throws a bridge over a strong stream is, of course, to build a great door to let the cat through, and little doors to let the kittens through; a great arch for the great current, to give it room in flood time, and little arches for the little currents along the shallow shore. This, even without any prudential

respect for the floods of the great current,
he would do in simple economy of work and
stone; for the smaller your arches are, the
less material you want on their flanks. Two
arches over the same span of river, supposing the butments are at the same depth, are
cheaper than one, and that by a great deal;
so that, where the current is shallow, the
village mason makes his arches many and
low: as the water gets deeper, and it becomes
troublesome to build his piers up from the
bottom, he throws his arches wider; at last
he comes to the deep stream, and, as he cannot
build at the bottom of that, he throws his
largest arch over it with a leap, and with
another little one or so gains the opposite
shore. Of course as arches are wider they
must be higher, or they will not stand; so the
roadway must rise as the arches widen. And
thus we have the general type of bridge, with
its highest and widest arch towards one side,
and a train of minor arches running over the
flat shore on the other: usually a steep bank
at the river-side next the large arch; always,
of course, a flat shore on the side of the small
ones: and the bend of the river assuredly

concave towards this flat, cutting round, with
a sweep into the steep bank; or, if there is
no steep bank, still assuredly cutting into the
shore at the steep end of the bridge.

Now this kind of bridge, sympathising, as
it does, with the spirit of the river, and marking the nature of the thing it has to deal
with and conquer, is the ideal of a bridge;
and all endeavours to do the thing in a grand
engineer's manner, with a level roadway and
equal arches, are barbarous; not only because
all monotonous forms are ugly in themselves,
but because the mind perceives at once that
there has been cost uselessly thrown away for
the sake of formality.[1]

---

[1] The cost of art in getting a bridge level is *always* lost,
for you must get up to the height of the central arch at any
rate, and you only can make the whole bridge level by
putting the hill farther back, and pretending to have got rid
of it when you have not, but have only wasted money in
building an unnecessary embankment. Of course, the bridge
should not be difficultly or dangerously steep, but the
necessary slope, whatever it may be, should be in the bridge
itself, as far as the bridge can take it, and not pushed aside
into the approach, as in our Waterloo road; the only
rational excuse for doing which is that when the slope must
be long it is inconvenient to put on a drag at the top of
the bridge, and that any restiveness of the horse is more
dangerous on the bridge than on the embankment. To this
I answer: first, it is not more dangerous in reality, though

204. Well, to return to our continuity. We
see that the Turnerian bridge in Fig. 32 is of
the absolutely perfect type, and is still farther
interesting by having its main arch crowned
by a watch-tower. But as I want you to note
especially what perhaps was not the case in
the real bridge, but is entirely Turner's doing,
you will find that though the arches diminish
gradually, not one is *regularly* diminished—
they are all of different shapes and sizes : you
cannot see this clearly in Fig. 32, but in the
larger diagram, Fig. 34, over leaf, you will with
ease. This is indeed also part of the ideal of
a bridge, because the lateral currents near the
shore are of course irregular in size, and a
simple builder would naturally vary his arches
accordingly ; and also, if the bottom was rocky,
build his piers where the rocks came. But it is

it looks so, for the bridge is always guarded by an effective
parapet, but the embankment is sure to have no parapet, or
only a useless rail ; and secondly, that it is better to have
the slope on the bridge and make the roadway wide in proportion, so as to be quite safe, because a little waste of space
on the river is no loss, but your wide embankment at the side
loses good ground ; and so my picturesque bridges are right
as well as beautiful, and I hope to see them built again some
day instead of the frightful straight-backed things which we
fancy are fine, and accept from the pontifical rigidities of the
engineering mind.

not as a part of bridge ideal, but as a necessity
of all noble composition, that this irregularity
is introduced by Turner.   It at once raises the
object thus treated from the lower or vulgar
unity of rigid law to the greater unity of clouds,
and waves, and trees, and human souls, each
different, each obedient, and each in harmonious
service.

4. THE LAW OF CURVATURE.

205. There is, however, another point to be
noticed in this bridge of Turner's.   Not only
does it slope away unequally at its sides, but
it slopes in a gradual though very subtle curve.
And if you substitute a straight line for this
curve (drawing one with a rule from the base
of the tower on each side to the ends of the
bridge, in Fig. 34, and effacing the curve), you
will instantly see that the design has suffered
grievously.   You may ascertain, by experiment,
that all beautiful objects whatsoever are thus terminated by delicately curved lines, except where
the straight line is indispensable to their use or
stability ; and that when a complete system of
straight lines, throughout the form, is necessary

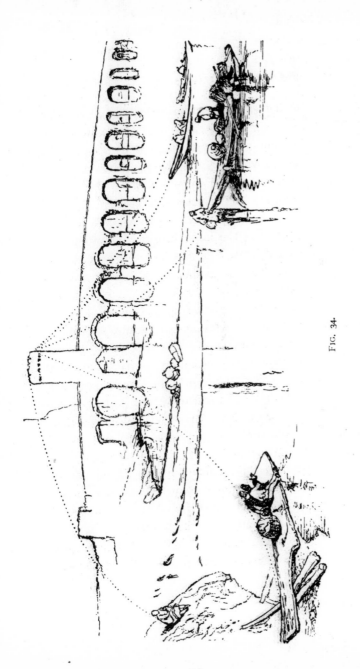

Fig. 34

to that stability, as in crystals, the beauty, if any exists, is in colour and transparency, not in form. Cut out the shape of any crystal you like, in white wax or wood, and put it beside a white lily, and you will feel the force of the curvature in its purity, irrespective of added colour, or other interfering elements of beauty.

206. Well, as curves are more beautiful than straight lines, it is necessary to a good composition that its continuities of object, mass, or colour should be, if possible, in curves, rather than straight lines or angular ones. Perhaps one of the simplest and prettiest examples of a graceful continuity of this kind is in the line traced at any moment by the corks of a net as it is being drawn : nearly every person is more or less attracted by the beauty of the dotted line. Now, it is almost always possible, not only to secure such a continuity in the arrangement or boundaries of objects which, like these bridge arches or the corks of the net, are actually connected with each other, but— and this is a still more noble and interesting kind of continuity—among features which appear at first entirely separate. Thus the towers of Ehrenbreitstein, on the left, in Fig. 32, appear

at first independent of each other; but when
I give their profile, on a larger scale, Fig. 35,
the reader may easily perceive that there is
a subtle cadence and harmony among them.

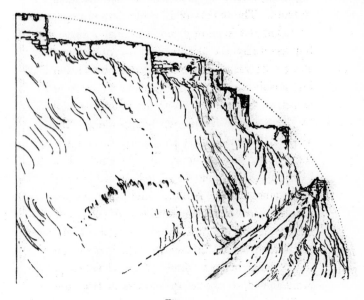

FIG. 35.

The reason of this is, that they are all bounded
by one grand curve, traced by the dotted line;
out of the seven towers, four precisely touch
this curve, the others only falling back from it

here and there to keep the eye from discovering
it too easily.

207. And it is not only always possible to
obtain continuities of this kind : it is, in drawing large forests or mountain forms, essential
to truth. The towers of Ehrenbreitstein might
or might not in reality fall into such a curve,
but assuredly the basalt rock on which they
stand did ; for all mountain forms not cloven
into absolute precipice, nor covered by straight
slopes of shales, are more or less governed
by these great curves, it being one of the
aims of Nature in all her work to produce
them. The reader must already know this,
if he has been able to sketch at all among
mountains ; if not, let him merely draw for
himself, carefully, the outlines of any low
hills accessible to him, where they are tolerably steep, or of the woods which grow on
them. The steeper shore of the Thames at
Maidenhead, or any of the downs at Brighton
or Dover, or, even nearer, about Croydon (as
Addington Hills), is easily accessible to a
Londoner ; and he will soon find not only
how constant, but how graceful the curvature
is. Graceful curvature is distinguished from

ungraceful by two characters; first in its
moderation, that is to say, its close approach
to straightness in some part of its course;[1]
and, secondly, by its variation, that is to say,
its never remaining equal in degree at different
parts of its course.

208. This variation is itself twofold in all
good curves.

A. There is, first, a steady change through

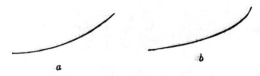

a   b

FIG. 36.

the whole line, from less to more curvature,
or more to less, so that *no* part of the line
is a segment of a circle, or can be drawn by
compasses in any way whatever. Thus, in
Fig. 36, *a* is a bad curve because it is
part of a circle, and is therefore monotonous
throughout; but *b* is a good curve, because

[1] I cannot waste space here by reprinting what I have
said in other books; but the reader ought, if possible, to
refer to the notices of this part of our subject in Modern
Painters, vol. iv. chap. xvii.; and Stones of Venice, vol. iii.
chap. i. § 8.

it continually changes its direction as it proceeds.

The *first* difference between good and bad
drawing of tree boughs consists in observance
of this fact. Thus, when I put leaves on
the line *b*, as in Fig. 37, you can immediately
feel the springiness of character dependent on
the changefulness of the curve. You may
put leaves on the other line for yourself, but
you will find you cannot make a right tree

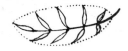

FIG. 37.

spray of it. For *all* tree boughs, large or
small, as well as all noble natural lines whatsoever, agree in this character; and it is a
point of primal necessity that your eye should
always seize and your hand trace it. Here
are two more portions of good curves, with
leaves put on them at the extremities instead
of the flanks, Fig. 38; and two showing
the arrangement of masses of foliage seen a
little farther off, Fig. 39, which you may in
like manner amuse yourself by turning into

segments of circles—you will see with what
result. I hope however you have beside

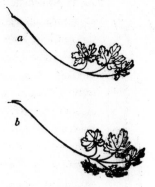

FIG. 38.

you, by this time, many good studies of tree
boughs carefully made, in which you may

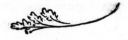

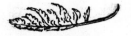

FIG. 39.

study variations of curvature in their mo...
complicated and lovely forms.[1]

[1] If you happen to be reading at this part of the boo...
without having gone through any previous practice, turn ba...

209. B. Not only does every good curve vary in general tendency, but it is modulated,

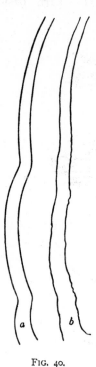

FIG. 40.

as it proceeds, by myriads of subordinate curves. Thus the outlines of a tree trunk are never as at *a*, Fig. 40, but as at *b*. So also in waves, clouds, and all other nobly formed masses. Thus another essential difference between good and bad drawing, or good and bad sculpture, depends on the quantity and refinement of minor curvatures carried, by good work, into the great lines. Strictly speaking, however, this is not variation in large curves, but composition of large curves out of small ones; it is an increase in the quantity of the beautiful element, but not a change in its nature.

to the sketch of the ramification of stone pine, Fig. 4, p. 29, and examine the curves of its boughs one by one, trying them by the conditions here stated under the heads A and B.

5. THE LAW OF RADIATION.

210. We have hitherto been concerned only
with the binding of our various objects into
beautiful lines or processions. The next point
we have to consider is, how we may unite
these lines or processions themselves, so as
to make groups of *them*.

Now, there are two kinds of harmonies of
lines. One in which, moving more or less
side by side, they variously, but evidently
with consent, retire from or approach each
other, intersect or oppose each other; currents
of melody in music, for different voices, thus
approach and cross, fall and rise, in harmony;
so the waves of the sea, as they approach the
shore, flow into one another or cross, but
with a great unity through all; and so various
lines of composition often flow harmoniously
through and across each other in a picture.
But the most simple and perfect connexion
of lines is by radiation; that is, by their all
springing from one point, or closing towards
it; and this harmony is often, in Nature
almost always, united with the other; as the

boughs of trees, though they intersect and play amongst each other irregularly, indicate by their general tendency their origin from one root. An essential part of the beauty of all vegetable form is in this radiation; it is seen most simply in a single flower or leaf, as in a convolvulus bell, or chestnut leaf; but more beautifully in the complicated arrangements of the large boughs and sprays. For a leaf is only a flat piece of radiation; but the tree throws its branches on all sides, and even in every profile view of it, which presents a radiation more or less correspondent to that of its leaves, it is more beautiful, because varied by the freedom of the separate branches. I believe it has been ascertained that, in all trees, the angle at which, in their leaves, the lateral ribs are set on their central rib is approximately the same at which the branches leave the great stem; and thus each section of the tree would present a kind of magnified view of its own leaf, were it not for the interfering force of gravity on the masses of foliage. This force in proportion to their age, and the lateral leverage upon them, bears them downwards at the extremities,

so that, as before noticed, the lower the
bough grows on the stem, the more it
droops (Fig. 17, p. 121); besides this, nearly
all beautiful trees have a tendency to divide
into two or more principal masses, which give
a prettier and more complicated symmetry than
if one stem ran all the way up the centre. Fig.
41 may thus be considered the simplest type

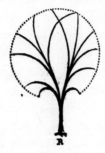

FIG. 41.

of tree radiation, as opposed to leaf radiation.
In this figure, however, all secondary ramification is unrepresented, for the sake of simplicity; but if we take one half of such a
tree, and merely give two secondary branches
to each main branch (as represented in the
general branch structure shown at *b*, Fig.
18, p. 122), we shall have the form Fig. 42.

S

This I consider the perfect general type of
tree structure; and it is curiously connected
with certain forms of Greek, Byzantine, and
Gothic ornamentation, into the discussion of

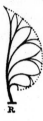

which, however, we must not enter
here. It will be observed, that both
in Figs. 41 and 42 all the branches
so spring from the main stem as
very nearly to suggest their united
radiation from the root R.   This is
by no means universally the case;
but if the branches do not bend
towards a point in the root, they
at least converge to some point or other.   In
the examples in Fig. 43, the mathematical
centre of curvature, a, is thus, in one case,
on the ground, at some distance from the
root, and in the other, near the top of the
tree.   Half, only, of each tree is given, for
the sake of clearness: Fig. 44 gives both
sides of another example, in which the origins
of curvature are below the root.   As the positions of such points may be varied without
end, and as the arrangement of the lines is
also farther complicated by the fact of the
boughs springing for the most part in a spiral

FIG. 42.

order round the tree, and at proportionate
distances, the systems of curvature which
regulate the form of vegetation are quite
infinite.   Infinite is a word easily said, and
easily written, and people do not always mean

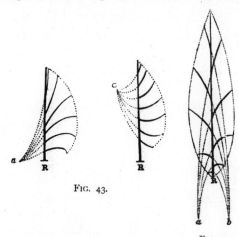

FIG. 43.

FIG. 44.

it when they say it; in this case I *do* mean
it: the number of systems is incalculable, and
even to furnish anything like a representative
number of types, I should have to give several
hundreds of figures such as Fig. 44.[1]

---

[1] The reader, I hope, observes always that every line in
these figures is itself one of varying curvature, and cannot
be drawn by compasses.

211. Thus far, however, we have only been speaking of the great relations of stem and branches. The forms of the branches themselves are regulated by still more subtle laws, for they occupy an intermediate position between the form of the tree and of the leaf. The leaf has a flat ramification; the tree a completely rounded one; the bough is neither rounded nor flat, but has a structure exactly balanced between the two, in a half-flattened, half-rounded flake, closely resembling in shape one of the thick leaves of an artichoke or the flake of a fir cone; by combination forming the solid mass of the tree, as the leaves compose the artichoke head. I have before pointed out to you the general resemblance of these branch flakes to an extended hand; but they may be more accurately represented by the ribs of a boat. If you can imagine a very broad-headed and flattened boat applied by its keel to the end of a main branch,[1] as in Fig.

[1] I hope the reader understands that these woodcuts are merely facsimiles of the sketches I make at the side of my paper to illustrate my meaning as I write—often sadly scrawled if I want to get on to something else. This one is really a little too careless; but it would take more time and trouble to make a proper drawing of so odd a boat than the matter is worth. It will answer the purpose well enough as it is.

45, the lines which its ribs will take, supposing them outside of its timbers instead of
inside, and the general contour of it, as seen
in different directions, from above and below,
will give you the closest approximation to the
perspectives and foreshortenings of a well-
grown branch-flake. Fig. 25 above, p. 160,
is an unharmed and unrestrained shoot of
healthy young oak; and, if you compare it
with Fig. 45, you will understand at once the

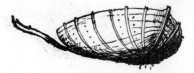

FIG. 45.

action of the lines of leafage; the boat only
failing as a type in that its ribs are too nearly
parallel to each other at the sides, while the
bough sends all its ramification well forwards,
rounding to the head, that it may accomplish
its part in the outer form of the whole tree,
yet always securing the compliance with the
great universal law that the branches nearest
the root bend most back; and, of course,
throwing *some* always back as well as

forwards; the appearance of reversed action being much increased, and rendered more striking and beautiful, by perspective. Fig. 25 shows the perspective of such a bough as it is seen from below; Fig. 46 gives rudely the look it would have from above.

212. You may suppose, if you have not already discovered, what subtleties of perspective and light and shade are involved in

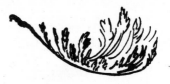

FIG. 46.

the drawing of thése branch-flakes, as you see them in different directions and actions; now raised, now depressed: touched on the edges by the wind, or lifted up and bent back so as to show all the white under surfaces of the leaves shivering in light, as the bottom of a boat rises white with spray at the surge-crest; or drooping in quietness towards the dew of the grass beneath them in windless mornings, or bowed down under oppressive grace of

deep-charged snow.   Snow time, by the way,
is one of the best for practice in the placing
of tree masses; but you will only be able to
understand them thoroughly by beginning
with a single bough and a few leaves placed
tolerably even, as in Fig. 38, p. 269. First
one with three leaves, a central and two
lateral ones, as at *a ;* then with five, as at *b*,
and so on ; directing your whole attention to
the expression, both by contour and light and
shade, of the boat-like arrangements, which,
in your earlier studies, will have been a good
deal confused, partly owing to your inexperience, and partly to the depth of shade,
or absolute blackness of mass required in
those studies.

213. One thing more remains to be noted,
and I will let you out of the wood. You see
that in every generally representative figure I
have surrounded the radiating branches with
a dotted line : such lines do indeed terminate
every vegetable form ; and you see that they
are themselves beautiful curves, which, according · to their flow, and the width or
narrowness of the spaces they enclose, char-
acterise the species of tree or leaf, and express

its free or formal action, its grace of youth or
weight of age.   So that, throughout all the
freedom of her wildest foliage, Nature is resolved on expressing an encompassing limit;
and marking a unity in the whole tree, caused
not only by the rising of its branches from
a common root, but by their joining in one
work, and being bound by a common law.
And having ascertained this, let us turn back
for a moment to a point in leaf structure
which, I doubt not, you must already have
observed in your earlier studies, but which it
is well to state here, as connected with the
unity of the branches in the great trees.   You
must have noticed, I should think, that whenever a leaf is compound,— that is to say,
divided into other leaflets which in any way
repeat or imitate the form of the whole leaf,
—those leaflets are not symmetrical, as the
whole leaf is, but always smaller on the side
towards the point of the great leaf, so as to
express their subordination to it, and show,
even when they are pulled off, that they are
not small independent leaves, but members of
one large leaf.

214. Fig. 47, which is a block-plan of a leaf

of columbine, without its minor divisions on
the edges, will illustrate the principle clearly.
It is composed of a central large mass, A, and
two lateral ones, of which the one on the right
only is lettered, B.   Each of these masses is

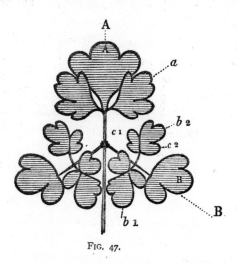

FIG. 47.

again composed of three others, a central and
two lateral ones; but observe, the minor one,
a of A, is balanced equally by its opposite;
but the minor *b* 1 of B is larger than its opposite *b* 2.   Again, each of these minor masses
is divided into three; but while the central

mass, A of A, is symmetrically divided, the
B of B is unsymmetrical, its largest side-lobe
being lowest. Again, in b 2, the lobe c 1 (its
lowest lobe in relation to B) is larger than c 2;
and so also in b 1. So that universally one
lobe of a lateral leaf is always larger than the
other, and the smaller lobe is that which is
nearer the central mass; the lower leaf, as it
were by courtesy, subduing some of its own
dignity or power, in the immediate presence
of the greater or captain leaf, and always
expressing, therefore, its own subordination
and secondary character. This law is carried
out even in single leaves. As far as I know,
the upper half, towards the point of the spray,
is always the smaller; and a slightly different
curve, more convex at the springing, is used
for the lower side, giving an exquisite variety
to the form of the whole leaf; so that one of
the chief elements in the beauty of every
subordinate leaf throughout the tree is made
to depend on its confession of its own lowliness
and subjection.

215. And now, if we bring together in one
view the principles we have ascertained in trees,
we shall find they may be summed under four

great laws; and that all perfect[1] vegetable form is appointed to express these four laws in noble balance of authority.

1. Support from one living root.

2. Radiation, or tendency of force from some one given point, either in the root, or in some stated connection with it.

3. Liberty of each bough to seek its own livelihood and happiness according to its needs, by irregularities of action both in its play and its work, either stretching out to get its required nourishment from light and rain, by finding some sufficient breathing-place among the other branches, or knotting and gathering itself up to get strength for any load which its fruitful blossoms may lay upon it, and for any stress of its storm-tossed luxuriance of leaves; or playing hither and thither as the fitful sunshine may tempt its young shoots, in their undecided states of mind about their future life.

---

[1] Imperfect vegetable form I consider that which is in its nature dependent, as in runners and climbers; or which is susceptible of continual injury without materially losing the power of giving pleasure by its aspect, as in the case of the smaller grasses. I have not, of course, space here to explain these minor distinctions, but the laws above stated apply to all the more important trees and shrubs likely to be familiar to the student.

4. Imperative requirement of each bough to stop within certain limits, expressive of its kindly fellowship and fraternity with the boughs in its neighbourhood; and to work with them according to its power, magnitude, and state of health, to bring out the general perfectness of the great curve, and circumferent stateliness of the whole tree.

216. I think I may leave you, unhelped, to work out the moral analogies of these laws; you may, perhaps, however, be a little puzzled to see the meaning of the second one. It typically expresses that healthy human actions should spring radiantly (like rays) from some single heart motive; the most beautiful systems of action taking place when this motive lies at the root of the whole life, and the action is clearly seen to proceed from it; while also many beautiful secondary systems of action taking place from motives not so deep or central, but in some beautiful subordinate connection with the central or life motive.

The other laws, if you think over them, you will find equally significative; and as you draw trees more and more in their various

states of health and hardship, you will be
every day more struck by the beauty of the
types they present of the truths most essential
for mankind to know; [1] and you will see what
this vegetation of the earth, which is necessary
to our life, first, as purifying the air for us and
then as food, and just as necessary to our joy
in all places of the earth,—what these trees
and leaves, I say, are meant to teach us as
we contemplate them, and read or hear their
lovely language, written or spoken for us, not
in frightful black letters nor in dull sentences,
but in fair green and shadowy shapes of waving

[1] There is a very tender lesson of this kind in the shadows
of leaves upon the ground; shadows which are the most
likely of all to attract attention, by their pretty play and
change. If you examine them, you will find that the shadows
do not take the forms of the leaves, but that, through each
interstice, the light falls, at a little distance, in the form of
a round or oval spot; that is to say, it produces the image of
the sun itself, cast either vertically or obliquely, in circle or
ellipse according to the slope of the ground. Of course the
sun's rays produce the same effect, when they fall through any
small aperture : but the openings between leaves are the only
ones likely to show it to an ordinary observer, or to attract his
attention to it by its frequency, and lead him to think what
this type may signify respecting the greater Sun; and how
it may show us that, even when the opening through which
the earth receives light is too small to let us see the Sun
Himself, the ray of light that enters, if it comes straight from
Him, will still bear with it His image.

words, and blossomed brightness of odoriferous wit, and sweet whispers of unintrusive wisdom, and playful morality.

217. Well, I am sorry myself to leave the wood, whatever my reader may be; but leave it we must, or we shall compose no more pictures to-day.

This law of radiation, then, enforcing unison of action in arising from, or proceeding to, some given point, is perhaps, of all principles of composition, the most influential in producing the beauty of groups of form. Other laws make them forcible or interesting, but this generally is chief in rendering them beautiful. In the arrangement of masses in pictures, it is constantly obeyed by the great composers; but, like the law of principality, with careful concealment of its imperativeness, the point to which the lines of main curvature are directed being very often far away out of the picture. Sometimes, however, a system of curves will be employed definitely to exalt, by their concurrence, the value of some leading object, and then the law becomes traceable enough.

218. In the instance before us, the principal

object being, as we have seen, the tower on
the bridge, Turner has determined that his
system of curvature should have its origin in
the top of this tower.   The diagram Fig. 34,
p. 263, compared with Fig. 32, p. 248, will
show how this is done.   One curve joins the
two towers, and is continued by the back of
the figure sitting on the bank into the piece
of bent timber.   This is a limiting curve of
great importance, and Turner has drawn a
considerable part of it with the edge of the
timber very carefully, and then led the eye up
to the sitting girl by some white spots and
indications of a ledge in the bank ; then the
passage to the tops of the towers cannot be
missed.

219. The next curve is begun and drawn
carefully for half an inch of its course by the
rudder ; it is then taken up by the basket and
the heads of the figures, and leads accurately
to the tower angle.   The gunwales of both
the boats begin the next two curves, which
meet in the same point ; and all are centralised
by the long reflection which continues the vertical lines.

220. Subordinated to this first system of

curves there is another, begun by the small
crossing bar of wood inserted in the angle
behind the rudder; continued by the bottom
of the bank on which the figure sits, interrupted forcibly beyond it,[1] but taken up again
by the water-line leading to the bridge foot,
and passing on in delicate shadows under the
arches, not easily shown in so rude a diagram,
towards the other extremity of the bridge.
This is a most important curve, indicating that
the force and sweep of the river have indeed
been in old times under the large arches;
while the antiquity of the bridge is told us by
a long tongue of land, either of carted rubbish,
or washed down by some minor stream, which
has interrupted this curve, and is now used as
a landing-place for the boats, and for embarka-
tion of merchandise, of which some bales and
bundles are laid in a heap, immediately beneath
the great tower.   A common composer would

[1] In the smaller figure (32), it will be seen that this inter-
ruption is caused by a cart coming down to the water's edge ;
and this object is serviceable as beginning another system of
curves leading out of the picture on the right, but so obscurely
drawn as not to be easily represented in outline. As it is
unnecessary to the explanation of our point here, it has been
omitted in the larger diagram, the direction of the curve it
begins being indicated by the dashes only.

have put these bales to one side or the other, but Turner knows better; he uses them as a foundation for his tower, adding to its importance precisely as the sculptured base adorns a pillar; and he farther increases the aspect of its height by throwing the reflection of it far down in the nearer water. All the great composers have this same feeling about sustaining their vertical masses: you will constantly find Prout using the artifice most dexterously (see, for instance, the figure with the wheelbarrow under the great tower, in the sketch of St. Nicholas, at Prague, and the white group of figures under the tower in the sketch of Augsburg[1]); and Veronese, Titian, and Tintoret continually put their principal figures at bases of pillars. Turner found out their secret very early, the most prominent instance of his composition on this principle being the drawing of Turin from the Superga, in Hakewell's Italy. I chose Fig. 20, already given to illustrate foliage drawing, chiefly because, being another instance of precisely the same arrangement, it will serve to convince you of its being intentional. There, the vertical, formed by the larger tree, is

[1] Both in the Sketches in Flanders and Germany.

T

continued by the figure of the farmer, and that
of one of the smaller trees by his stick.   The
lines of the interior mass of the bushes radiate,
under the law of radiation, from a point behind
the farmer's head ; but their outline curves are
carried on and repeated, under the law of continuity, by the curves of the dog and boy—
by the way, note the remarkable instance in
these of the use of darkest lines towards the
light—all more or less guiding the eye up to the
right, in order to bring it finally to the Keep
of Windsor, which is the central object of the
picture, as the bridge tower is in the Coblentz.
The wall on which the boy climbs answers the
purpose of contrasting, both in direction and
character, with these greater curves ; thus corresponding as nearly as possible to the minor
tongue of land in the Coblentz.   This, however, introduces us to another law, which we
must consider separately.

6. THE LAW OF CONTRAST.

221. Of course the character of everything is
best manifested by Contrast.   Rest can only
be enjoyed after labour; sound to be heard

clearly, must rise out of silence; light is exhibited by darkness, darkness by light; and so
on in all things.   Now in art every colour has
an opponent colour, which, if brought near it,
will relieve it more completely than any other;
so, also, every form and line may be made
more striking to the eye by an opponent form
or line near them; a curved line is set off by a
straight one, a massy form by a slight one, and
so on; and in all good work nearly double the
value, which any given colour or form would
have uncombined, is given to each by contrast.[1]

In this case again, however, a too manifest
use of the artifice vulgarises a picture.   Great
painters do not commonly, or very visibly, admit
violent contrast.   They introduce it by stealth,
and with intermediate links of tender change;
allowing, indeed, the opposition to tell upon the
mind as a surprise, but not as a shock.[2]

[1] If you happen to meet with the plate of Dürer's representing a coat-of-arms with a skull in the shield, note the value
given to the concave curves and sharp point of the helmet by
the convex leafage carried round it in front; and the use of
the blank white part of the shield in opposing the rich folds
of the dress.

[2] Turner hardly ever, as far as I remember, allows a strong
light to oppose a full dark, without some intervening tint.
His suns never set behind dark mountains without a film of
cloud above the mountain's edge.

222. Thus in the rock of Ehrenbreitstein, Fig. 35, the main current of the lines being downwards, in a convex swell, they are suddenly stopped at the lowest tower by a counter series of beds, directed nearly straight across them.   This adverse force sets off and relieves the great curvature, but it is reconciled to it by a series of radiating lines below, which at first sympathise with the oblique bar, then gradually get steeper, till they meet and join in the fall of the great curve.   No passage, however intentionally monotonous, is ever introduced by a good artist without *some* slight counter current of this kind; so much, indeed, do the great composers feel the necessity of it, that they will even do things purposely ill or unsatisfactorily, in order to give greater value to their well-doing in other places.   In a skilful poet's versification the so-called bad or inferior lines are not inferior because he could not do them better, but because he feels that if all were equally weighty, there would be no real sense of weight anywhere; if all were equally melodious, the melody itself would be fatiguing; and he purposely introduces the labouring or discordant verse, that the full

ring may be felt in his main sentence, and the finished sweetness in his chosen rhythm.[1] And continually in painting, inferior artists destroy their work by giving too much of all that they think is good, while the great painter gives just enough to be enjoyed, and passes to an opposite kind of enjoyment, or to an inferior state of enjoyment: he gives a passage of rich, involved, exquisitely wrought colour, then passes away into slight, and pale, and simple colour; he paints for a minute or two with intense decision, then suddenly becomes, as the spectator thinks, slovenly; but he is not slovenly: you could not have *taken* any more decision from him just then; you have had as much as is good for you: he paints over a great space of his picture forms of the most rounded and melting tenderness, and suddenly, as you think by a freak, gives you a bit as jagged and sharp

---

[1] " A prudent chief not always must display
His powers in equal ranks and fair array,
But with the occasion and the place comply,
Conceal his force; nay, seem sometimes to fly.
Those oft are stratagems which errors seem,
Nor is it Homer nods, but we that dream."
                                        Essay on Criticism.

as a leafless blackthorn.   Perhaps the most
exquisite piece of subtle contrast in the world
of painting is the arrow point, laid sharp against
the white side and among the flowing hair of
Correggio's Antiope.   It is quite singular how
very little contrast will sometimes serve to

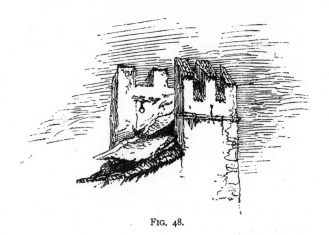

FIG. 48.

make an entire group of forms interesting
which would otherwise have been valueless.
There is a good deal of picturesque material,
for instance, in this top of an old tower,
Fig. 48, tiles and stones and sloping roof not
disagreeably mingled ; but all would have been

unsatisfactory if there had not happened to be
that iron ring on the inner wall, which by its
vigorous black *circular* line precisely opposes
all the square and angular characters of the
battlements and roof. Draw the tower without
the ring, and see what a difference it will
make.

223. One of the most important applications
of the law of contrast is in association with the
law of continuity, causing an unexpected but
gentle break in a continuous series. This
artifice is perpetual in music, and perpetual
also in good illumination ; the way in which
little surprises of change are prepared in any
current borders, or chains of ornamental design,
being one of the most subtle characteristics of
the work of the good periods. We take, for
instance, a bar of ornament between two written
columns of an early fourteenth century MS.,
and at the first glance we suppose it to be
quite monotonous all the way up, composed of
a winding tendril, with alternately a blue leaf
and a scarlet bud. Presently, however, we see
that, in order to observe the law of principality,
there is one large scarlet leaf instead of a bud,
nearly half-way up, which forms a centre to

the whole rod ; and when we begin to examine the order of the leaves, we find it varied carefully.   Let A stand for scarlet bud, *b* for blue leaf, *c* for two blue leaves on one stalk, *s* for a stalk without a leaf, and R for the large red leaf.   Then, counting from the ground, the order begins as follows :

b, *b*, A ; *b*, *s*, *b*, A ; *b*, *b*, A ; *b*, *b*, A ; and we think we shall have two *b*'s and an A all the way, when suddenly it becomes *b*, A ; *b*, R ; *b*, A ; *b*, A ; *b*, A ; and we think we are going to have *b*, A continued ; but no : here it becomes *b*, *s* ; *b*, *s* ; *b*, A ; *b*, *s* ; *b*, *s* ; *c*, *s* ; *b*, *s* ; *b*, *s* ; and we think we are surely going to have *b*, *s* continued, but behold it runs away to the end with a quick *b*, *b*, A ; *b*, *b*, *b*, *b* /[1]   Very often, however, the designer is satisfied with *one* surprise, but I never saw a good illuminated border without one at least ; and no series of any kind was ever introduced by a great composer in a painting without a snap somewhere.   There is a pretty one in Turner's drawing of Rome with the large balustrade for a foreground in the Hakewell's Italy series :

[1] I am describing from an MS., *circa* 1300, of Gregory's Decretalia, in my own possession.

the single baluster struck out of the line, and
showing the street below through the gap,
simply makes the whole composition right,
when otherwise it would have been stiff and
absurd.

224. If you look back to Fig. 48 you will
see, in the arrangement of the battlements,
a simple instance of the use of such variation.
The whole top of the tower, though actually
three sides of a square, strikes the eye as a
continuous series of five masses.   The first
two, on the left, somewhat square and blank,
then the next two higher and richer, the tiles
being seen on their slopes.   Both these groups
being couples, there is enough monotony in the
series to make a change pleasant; and the last
battlement, therefore, is a little higher than the
first two,—a little lower than the second two,
—and different in shape from either.   Hide it
with your finger, and see how ugly and formal
the other four battlements look.

225. There are in this figure several other
simple illustrations of the laws we have been
tracing.   Thus the whole shape of the walls'
mass being square, it is well, still for the sake of
contrast, to oppose it not only by the element

of curvature, in the ring, and lines of the roof
below, but by that of sharpness ; hence the
pleasure which the eye takes in the projecting
point of the roof. Also, because the walls are
thick and sturdy, it is well to contrast their
strength with weakness; therefore we enjoy
the evident decrepitude of this roof as it sinks
between them. The whole mass being nearly
white, we want a contrasting shadow somewhere ; and get it, under our piece of decrepitude. This shade, with the tiles of the wall
below, forms another pointed mass, necessary
to the first by the law of repetition. Hide this
inferior angle with your finger, and see how
ugly the other looks. A sense of the law of
symmetry, though you might hardly suppose
it, has some share in the feeling with which
you look at the battlements; there is a certain
pleasure in the opposed slopes of their top,
on one side down to the left, on the other to
the right. Still less would you think the law
of radiation had anything to do with the matter :
but if you take the extreme point of the black
shadow on the left for a centre, and follow first
the low curve of the eaves of the wall, it will
lead you, if you continue it, to the point of the

tower cornice; follow the second curve, the
top of the tiles of the wall, and it will strike
the top of the right-hand battlement; then
draw a curve from the highest point of the
angled battlement on the left, through the points
of the roof and its dark echo; and you will
see how the whole top of the tower radiates
from this lowest dark point.   There are other
curvatures crossing these main ones, to keep
them from being too conspicuous.   Follow the
curve of the upper roof, it will take you to
the top of the highest battlement; and the
stones indicated at the right-hand side of the
tower are more extended at the bottom, in
order to get some less direct expression of
sympathy, such as irregular stones may be
capable of, with the general flow of the curves
from left to right.

226. You may not readily believe, at first,
that all these laws are indeed involved in so
trifling a piece of composition.   But, as you
study longer, you will discover that these laws,
and many more, are obeyed by the powerful
composers in every *touch :* that literally, there
is never a dash of their pencil which is not
carrying out appointed purposes of this kind in

twenty various ways at once; and that there
is as much difference, in way of intention and
authority, between one of the great composers
ruling his colours, and a common painter confused by them, as there is between a general
directing the march of an army, and an old
lady carried off her feet by a mob.

7. THE LAW OF INTERCHANGE.

227. Closely connected with the law of contrast is a law which enforces the unity of
opposite things, by giving to each a portion
of the character of the other. If, for instance,
you divide a shield into two masses of colour,
all the way down—suppose blue and white,
and put a bar, or figure of an animal, partly
on one division, partly on the other, you will
find it pleasant to the eye if you make the part
of the animal blue which comes upon the white
half, and white which comes upon the blue half.
This is done in heraldry, partly for the sake
of perfect intelligibility, but yet more for the
sake of delight in interchange of colour, since,
in all ornamentation whatever, the practice is
continual, in the ages of good design.

228. Sometimes this alternation is merely a reversal of contrasts; as that, after red has been for some time on one side, and blue on the other, red shall pass to blue's side and blue to red's. This kind of alternation takes place simply in four-quartered shields ; in more subtle pieces of treatment, a little bit only of each colour is carried into the other, and they are as it were dovetailed together. One of the most curious facts which will impress itself upon you, when you have drawn some time carefully from Nature in light and shade, is the appearance of intentional artifice with which contrasts of this alternate kind are produced by her ; the artistry with which she will darken a tree trunk as long as it comes against light sky, and throw sunlight on it precisely at the spot where it comes against a dark hill, and similarly treat all her masses of shade and colour, is so great, that if you only follow her closely, every one who looks at your drawing with attention will think that you have been inventing the most artificially and unnaturally delightful interchanges of shadow that could possibly be devised by human wit.

229. You will find this law of interchange

insisted upon at length by Prout in his Lessons on Light and Shade : it seems of all his principles of composition to be the one he is most conscious of; many others he obeys by instinct, but this he formally accepts and forcibly declares.

The typical purpose of the law of interchange is, of course, to teach us how opposite natures may be helped and strengthened by receiving each, as far as they can, some impress or reflection, or imparted power, from the other.

8. THE LAW OF CONSISTENCY.

230. It is to be remembered, in the next place, that while contrast exhibits the *characters* of things, it very often neutralises or paralyses their *power*. A number of white things may be shown to be clearly white by opposition of a black thing, but if we want the full power of their gathered light, the black thing may be seriously in our way.   Thus, while contrast displays things, it is unity and sympathy which employ them, concentrating the power of several into a mass.   And, not in art merely, but in all the affairs of life, the

wisdom of man is continually called upon to
reconcile these opposite methods of exhibiting,
or using, the materials in his power. By
change he gives them pleasantness, and by
consistency value; by change he is refreshed,
and by perseverance strengthened.

231. Hence many compositions address
themselves to the spectator by aggregate force
of colour or line, more than by contrasts of
either; many noble pictures are painted almost
exclusively in various tones of red, or grey,
or gold, so as to be instantly striking by their
breadth of flush, or glow, or tender coldness,
these qualities being exhibited only by slight
and subtle use of contrast. Similarly as to
form; some compositions associate massive
and rugged forms, others slight and graceful
ones, each with few interruptions by lines of
contrary character. And, in general, such
compositions possess higher sublimity than
those which are more mingled in their elements. They tell a special tale, and summon
a definite state of feeling, while the grand
compositions merely please the eye.

232. This unity or breadth of character
generally attaches most to the works of the

greatest men; their separate pictures have all
separate aims.   We have not, in each, grey
colour set against sombre, and sharp forms
against soft, and loud passages against low:
but we have the bright picture, with its delicate sadness; the sombre picture, with its
single ray of relief; the stern picture, with
only one tender group of lines; the soft and
calm picture, with only one rock angle at its
flank; and so on.   Hence the variety of their
work, as well as its impressiveness.   The
principal bearing of this law, however, is on
the separate masses or divisions of a picture:
the character of the whole composition may
be broken or various, if we please, but there
must certainly be a tendency to consistent
assemblage in its divisions.   As an army may
act on several points at once, but can only
act effectually by having somewhere formed
and regular masses, and not wholly by skir-
mishers; so a picture may be various in its
tendencies, but must be somewhere united
and coherent in its masses.   Good composers are always associating their colours
in great groups; binding their forms together
by encompassing lines, and securing, by

various dexterities of expedient, what they
themselves call "breadth:" that is to say,
a large gathering of each kind of thing into
one place; light being gathered to light,
darkness to darkness, and colour to colour.
If, however, this be done by introducing false
lights or false colours, it is absurd and mon-
strous; the skill of a painter consists in obtaining breadth by rational arrangement of
his objects, not by forced or wanton treatment
of them. It is an easy matter to paint one
thing all white, and another all black or
brown; but not an easy matter to assemble
all the circumstances which will naturally produce white in one place, and brown in another.
Generally speaking, however, breadth will result in sufficient degree from fidelity of study:
Nature is always broad; and if you paint
her colours in true relations, you will paint
them in majestic masses. If you find your
work look broken and scattered, it is, in
all probability, not only ill composed, but
untrue.

233. The opposite quality to breadth, that
of division or scattering of light and colour,
has a certain contrasting charm, and is

U

occasionally introduced with exquisite effect by good composers.[1] Still it is never the mere scattering, but the order discernible through this scattering, which is the real source of pleasure ; not the mere multitude, but the constellation of multitude. The broken lights in the work of a good painter wander like flocks upon the hills, not unshepherded, speaking of life and peace : the broken lights of a bad painter fall like hailstones, and are capable only of mischief, leaving it to be wished they were also of dissolution.

9. THE LAW OF HARMONY.

234. This last law is not, strictly speaking, so much one of composition as of truth, but it must guide composition, and is properly, therefore, to be stated in this place.

Good drawing is, as we have seen, an *abstract* of natural facts ; you cannot represent all that you would, but must continually be

---

[1] One of the most wonderful compositions of Tintoret in Venice, is little more than a field of subdued crimson, spotted with flakes of scattered gold. The upper clouds in the most beautiful skies owe great part of their power to infinitude of division ; order being marked through this division.

falling short, whether you will or no, of the force, or quantity, of Nature. Now, suppose that your means and time do not admit of your giving the depth of colour in the scene, and that you are obliged to paint it paler. If you paint all the colours proportionately paler, as if an equal quantity of tint had been washed away from each of them, you still obtain a harmonious, though not an equally forcible, statement of natural fact. But if you take away the colours unequally, and leave some tints nearly as deep as they are in Nature, while others are much subdued, you have no longer a true statement. You cannot say to the observer, " Fancy all those colours a little deeper, and you will have the actual fact." However he adds in imagination, or takes away, something is sure to be still wrong. The picture is out of harmony.

235. It will happen, however, much more frequently, that you have to darken the whole system of colours, than to make them paler. You remember, in your first studies of colour from Nature, you were to leave the passages of light which were too bright to be imitated, as white paper. But, in completing the picture,

it becomes necessary to put colour into them;
and then the other colours must be made darker,
in some fixed relation to them. If you deepen
all proportionately, though the whole scene is
darker than reality, it is only as if you were
looking at the reality in a lower light : but if,
while you darken some of the tints, you leave
others undarkened, the picture is out of harmony, and will not give the impression of
truth.

236. It is not, indeed, possible to deepen *all*
the colours so much as to relieve the lights in
their natural degree, you would merely sink
most of your colours, if you tried to do so,
into a broad mass of blackness : but it is
quite possible to lower them harmoniously,
and yet more in some parts of the picture than
in others, so as to allow you to show the light
you want in a visible relief. In well-har-
monised pictures this is done by gradually
deepening the tone of the picture towards the
lighter parts of it, without materially lowering
it in the very dark parts; the tendency in such
pictures being, of course, to include large
masses of middle tints. But the principal
point to be observed in doing this, is to deepen

the individual tints without dirtying or obscur-
ing them. It is easy to lower the tone of the
picture by washing it over with grey or brown ;
and easy to see the effect of the landscape,
when its colours are thus universally polluted
with black, by using the black convex mirror,
one of the most pestilent inventions for falsify-
ing Nature and degrading art which ever was
put into an artist's hand.[1] For the thing
required is not to darken pale yellow by mixing
grey with it, but to deepen the pure yellow ;
not to darken crimson by mixing black with
it, but by making it deeper and richer crimson :
and thus the required effect could only be seen
in Nature, if you had pieces of glass of the
colour of every object in your landscape, and
of every minor hue that made up those colours,
and then could see the real landscape through
this deep gorgeousness of the varied glass.
You cannot do this with glass, but you can
do it for yourself as you work ; that is to say,

---

[1] I fully believe that the strange grey gloom, accompanied
by considerable power of effect, which prevails in modern
French art, must be owing to the use of this mischievous
instrument ; the French landscape always gives me the idea
of Nature seen carelessly in the dark mirror, and painted
coarsely, but scientifically, through the veil of its perversion.

you can put deep blue for pale blue, deep gold for pale gold, and so on, in the proportion you need; and then you may paint as forcibly as you choose, but your work will still be in the manner of Titian, not of Caravaggio or Spagnoletto, or any other of the black slaves of painting.[1]

237. Supposing those scales of colour, which I told you to prepare in order to show you the relations of colour to grey, were quite accurately made, and numerous enough, you would have nothing more to do, in order to obtain a deeper tone in any given mass of colour, than to substitute for each of its hues the hue as many degrees deeper in the scale as you wanted, that is to say, if you wanted to deepen the whole two degrees, substituting for the yellow No. 5 the yellow No. 7, and for the red No. 9 the red No. 11, and so on: but the hues of any object in Nature are far too numerous, and their degrees too subtle, to admit of so mechanical a process.   Still, you may see the principle of the whole matter

---

[1] Various other parts of this subject are entered into, especially in their bearing on the ideal of painting, in Modern Painters, vol. iv. chap. iii.

clearly by taking a group of colours out of your scale, arranging them prettily, and then washing them all over with grey: that represents the treatment of Nature by the black mirror. Then arrange the same group of colours, with the tints five or six degrees deeper in the scale; and that will represent the treatment of Nature by Titian.

238. You can only, however, feel your way fully to the right of the thing by working from Nature.

The best subject on which to begin a piece of study of this kind is a good thick tree trunk, seen against blue sky with some white clouds in it. Paint the clouds in true and tenderly gradated white; then give the sky a bold full blue, bringing them well out; then paint the trunk and leaves grandly dark against all, but in such glowing dark green and brown as you see they will bear. Afterwards proceed to more complicated studies, matching the colours carefully first by your old method; then deepening each colour with its own tint, and being careful, above all things, to keep truth of equal change when the colours are connected with each other, as in dark and light sides of the same object. Much more aspect and sense of harmony are gained by the precision with which you observe the relation of colours in dark sides and light sides, and the influence of modifying reflections, than by mere accuracy of added depth in independent colours.

239. This harmony of tone, as it is generally called, is the most important of those which the artist has to regard. But there are all kinds of harmonies in a picture, according to its mode of production. There is even a harmony of touch. If you paint one part of it very rapidly and forcibly, and another part slowly and delicately, each division of the picture may be right separately, but they will not agree together: the whole will be effectless and valueless, out of harmony. Similarly, if you paint one part of it by a yellow light in a warm day, and another by a grey light in a cold day, though both may have been sunlight, and both may be well toned, and have their relative shadows truly cast, neither will look like light; they will destroy each other's power, by being out of harmony. These are only broad and

definable instances of discordance ; but there is
an extent of harmony in all good work much
too subtle for definition ; depending on the
draughtsman's carrying everything he draws
up to just the balancing and harmonious point,
in finish, and colour, and depth of tone, and
intensity of moral feeling, and style of touch,
all considered at once ; and never allowing
himself to lean too emphatically on detached
parts, or exalt one thing at the expense of
another, or feel acutely in one place and coldly
in another. If you have got some of Cruikshank's etchings, you will be able, I think,
to feel the nature of harmonious treatment in
a simple kind, by comparing them with any of
Richter's illustrations to the numerous German
story-books lately published at Christmas, with
all the German stories spoiled. Cruikshank's
work is often incomplete in character and poor
in incident, but, as drawing, it is *perfect* in
harmony. The pure and simple effects of day-
light which he gets by his thorough mastery
of treatment in this respect, are quite unrivalled, as far as I know, by any other
work executed with so few touches. His vignettes to Grimm's German stories, already

recommended, are the most remarkable in this quality.   Richter's illustrations, on the contrary, are of a very high stamp as respects understanding of human character, with infinite playfulness and tenderness of fancy; but, as drawings, they are almost unendurably out of harmony, violent blacks in one place being continually opposed to trenchant white in another; and, as is almost sure to be the case with bad harmonists, the local colour hardly felt anywhere.   All German work is apt to be out of harmony, in consequence of its too frequent conditions of affectation, and its wilful refusals of fact; as well as by reason of a feverish kind of excitement, which dwells violently on particular points, and makes all the lines of thought in the picture to stand on end, as it were, like a cat's fur electrified; while good work is always as quiet as a couchant leopard, and as strong.

240. I have now stated to you all the laws of composition which occur to me as capable of being illustrated or defined; but there are multitudes of others which, in the present state of my knowledge, I cannot define, and

others which I never hope to define ; and
these the most important, and connected with
the deepest powers of the art.   I hope, when
I have thought of them more, to be able to
explain some of the laws which relate to
nobleness and ignobleness ; that ignobleness
especially which we commonly call " vulgarity,"
and which, in its essence, is one of the most
curious subjects of inquiry connected with
human feeling.   Others I never hope to explain, laws of expression, bearing simply on
simple matters ; but, for that very reason,
more influential than any others.   These are,
from the first, as inexplicable as our bodily
sensations are; it being just as impossible, I
think, to show, finally, why one succession
of musical notes [1] shall be lofty and pathetic,
and such as might have been sung by Casella
to Dante, and why another succession is base
and ridiculous, and would be fit only for the

---

[1] In all the best arrangements of colour, the delight occa-
sioned by their mode of succession is entirely inexplicable, nor
can it be reasoned about ; we like it just as we like an air in
music, but cannot reason any refractory person into liking it,
if they do not : and yet there is distinctly a right and a wrong
in it, and a good taste and bad taste respecting it, as also
in music.

reasonably good ear of Bottom, as to explain why we like sweetness, and dislike bitterness. The best part of every great work is always inexplicable: it is good because it is good; and innocently gracious, opening as the green of the earth, or falling as the dew of heaven.

241. But though you cannot explain them, you may always render yourself more and more sensitive to these higher qualities by the discipline which you generally give to your character, and this especially with regard to the choice of incidents; a kind of composition in some sort easier than the artistical arrangements of lines and colours, but in every sort nobler, because addressed to deeper feelings.

242. For instance, in the "Datur Hora Quieti," the last vignette to Rogers's Poems, the plough in the foreground has three purposes. The first purpose is to meet the stream of sunlight on the river, and make it brighter by opposition; but any dark object whatever would have done this. Its second purpose is, by its two arms, to repeat the cadence of the group of the two ships, and thus give a greater expression of repose; but

two sitting figures would have done this. Its third and chief, or pathetic, purpose is, as it lies abandoned in the furrow (the vessels also being moored, and having their sails down), to be a type of human labour closed with the close of day. The parts of it on which the hand leans are brought most clearly into sight; and they are the chief dark of the picture, because the tillage of the ground is required of man as a punishment: but they make the soft light of the setting sun brighter, because rest is sweetest after toil. These thoughts may never occur to us as we glance carelessly at the design; and yet their under current assuredly affects the feelings, and increases, as the painter meant it should, the impression of melancholy, and of peace.

243. Again, in the "Lancaster Sands," which is one of the plates I have marked as most desirable for your possession: the stream of light which falls from the setting sun on the advancing tide stands similarly in need of some force of near object to relieve its brightness. But the incident which Turner has here adopted is the swoop of an angry sea-gull at a dog, who yelps at it, drawing back as the wave

rises over his feet, and the bird shrieks within a foot of his face. Its unexpected bold-ness is a type of the anger of its ocean element, and warns us of the sea's advance just as surely as the abandoned plough told us of the ceased labour of the day.

244. It is not, however, so much in the selection of single incidents of this kind, as in the feeling which regulates the arrange-ment of the whole subject, that the mind of a great composer is known. A single incident may be suggested by a felicitous chance, as a pretty motto might be for the heading of a chapter. But the great composers so arrange *all* their designs that one incident illustrates another, just as one colour relieves another. Perhaps the "Heysham," of the Yorkshire series, which, as to its locality, may be con-sidered a companion to the last drawing we have spoken of, the "Lancaster Sands," pre-sents as interesting an example as we could find of Turner's feeling in this respect. The subject is a simple north-country village, on the shore of Morecambe Bay; not in the common sense a picturesque village; there are no pretty bow-windows, or red roofs, or

rocky steps of entrance to the rustic doors, or quaint gables; nothing but a single street of thatched and chiefly clay-built cottages, ranged in a somewhat monotonous line, the roofs so green with moss that at first we hardly discern the houses from the fields and trees. The village street is closed at the end by a wooden gate, indicating the little traffic there is on the road through it, and giving it something the look of a large farmstead, in which a right of way lies through the yard. The road which leads to this gate is full of ruts, and winds down a bad bit of hill between two broken banks of moor ground, succeeding immediately to the few enclosures which surround the village; they can hardly be called gardens: but a decayed fragment or two of fencing fill the gaps in the bank; a clothes-line, with some clothes on it, striped blue and red, and a smock-frock, is stretched between the trunks of some stunted willows; a *very* small haystack and pig-stye being seen at the back of the cottage beyond. An empty, two-wheeled, lumbering cart, drawn by a pair of horses with huge wooden collars, the driver sitting lazily in the sun, sideways on the leader, is going slowly home along the rough road, it being about country dinner-time. At the end of the village there is a better house, with three chimneys and a dormer window in its roof, and the roof is of stone shingle instead of thatch, but very rough. This house is no doubt the clergyman's : there is some smoke from one of its chimneys, none from any other in the village; this smoke is from the lowest chimney at the back, evidently that of the kitchen, and it is rather thick, the fire not having been long lighted. A few hundred yards from the clergyman's house, nearer the shore, is the church, discernible from the cottages only by its low two-arched belfry, a little neater than one would expect in such a village; perhaps lately built by the Puseyite incumbent : [1] and beyond the church, close to the sea, are two fragments of a border war-tower, standing

---

[1] " Puseyism " was unknown in the days when this draw-ing was made ; but the kindly and helpful influences of what may be called ecclesiastical sentiment, which, in a morbidly exaggerated condition, forms one of the principal elements of " Puseyism,"—I use this word regretfully, no other exist-ing which will serve for it,—had been known and felt in our wild northern districts long before.

on their circular mound, worn on its brow deep into edges and furrows by the feet of the village children. On the bank of moor, which forms the foreground, are a few cows, the carter's dog barking at a vixenish one: the milkmaid is feeding another, a gentle white one, which turns its head to her, expectant of a handful of fresh hay, which she has brought for it in her blue apron, fastened up round her waist; she stands with her pail on her head, evidently the village coquette, for she has a neat bodice, and pretty striped petticoat under the blue apron, and red stockings. Nearer us, the cowherd, barefooted, stands on a piece of the limestone rock (for the ground is thistly and not pleasurable to bare feet);—whether boy or girl we are not sure: it may be a boy, with a girl's worn-out bonnet on, or a girl with a pair of ragged trowsers on; probably the first, as the old bonnet is evidently useful to keep the sun out of our eyes when we are looking for strayed cows among the moorland hollows, and helps us at present to watch (holding the bonnet's edge down) the quarrel of the vixenish cow with the dog, which, leaning on our long

x

stick, we allow to proceed without any interference.   A little to the right the hay is being
got in, of which the milkmaid has just taken
her apronful to the white cow; but the hay
is very thin, and cannot well be raked up
because of the rocks; we must glean it like
corn, hence the smallness of our stack behind
the willows; and a woman is pressing a
bundle of it hard together, kneeling against
the rock's edge, to carry it safely to the hay-
cart without dropping any.   Beyond the village is a rocky hill, deep set with brushwood,
a square crag or two of limestone emerging
here and there, with pleasant turf on their
brows, heaved in russet and mossy mounds
against the sky, which, clear and calm, and
as golden as the moss, stretches down behind
it towards the sea.   A single cottage just
shows its roof over the edge of the hill, looking seawards: perhaps one of the village
shepherds is a sea captain now, and may have
built it there, that his mother may first see
the sails of his ship whenever it runs into
the bay.   Then under the hill, and beyond
the border tower, is the blue sea itself, the
waves flowing in over the sand in long curved

lines slowly; shadows of cloud, and gleams
of shallow water on white sand alternating—
miles away; but no sail is visible, not one
fisher-boat on the beach, not one dark speck
on the quiet horizon.   Beyond all are the
Cumberland mountains, clear in the sun, with
rosy light on all their crags.

245. I should think the reader cannot but
feel the kind of harmony there is in this composition; the entire purpose of the painter to
give us the impression of wild, yet gentle,
country life, monotonous as the succession of
the noiseless waves, patient and enduring as
the rocks; but peaceful, and full of health
and quiet hope, and sanctified by the pure
mountain air and baptismal dew of heaven,
falling softly between days of toil and nights
of innocence.

246. All noble composition of this kind can be
reached only by instinct; you cannot set yourself to arrange such a subject; you may see
it, and seize it, at all times, but never labori-
ously invent it.   And your power of discerning what is best in expression, among natural
subjects, depends wholly on the temper in
which you keep your own mind; above all,

on your living so much alone as to allow it to
become acutely sensitive in its own stillness.
The noisy life of modern days is wholly in-
compatible with any true perception of natural
beauty. If you go down into Cumberland by
the railroad, live in some frequented hotel, and
explore the hills with merry companions, however much you may enjoy your tour or their
conversation, depend upon it you will never
choose so much as one pictorial subject rightly ;
you will not see into the depth of any. But
take knapsack and stick, walk towards the
hills by short day's journeys,—ten or twelve
miles a day—taking a week from some start-
ing-place sixty or seventy miles away : sleep
at the pretty little wayside inns, or the rough
village ones ; then take the hills as they tempt
you, following glen or shore as your eye
glances or your heart guides, wholly scornful
of local fame or fashion, and of everything
which it is the ordinary traveller's duty to
see, or pride to do. Never force yourself to
admire anything when you are not in the
humour ; but never force yourself away from
what you feel to be lovely, in search of anything better ; and gradually the deeper scenes

of the natural world will unfold themselves to you in still increasing fulness of passionate power; and your difficulty will be no more to seek or to compose subjects, but only to choose one from among the multitude of melodious thoughts with which you will be haunted, thoughts which will of course be noble or original in proportion to your own depth of character and general power of mind; for it is not so much by the consideration you give to any single drawing, as by the previous discipline of your powers of thought, that the character of your composition will be determined.   Simplicity of life will make you sensitive to the refinement and modesty of scenery, just as inordinate excitement and pomp of daily life will make you enjoy coarse colours and affected forms.   Habits of patient comparison and accurate judgment will make your art precious, as they will make your actions wise; and every increase of noble enthusiasm in your living spirit will be measured by the reflection of its light upon the works of your hands.—Faithfully yours,

J. RUSKIN.

APPENDIX.

APPENDIX.

I.

ILLUSTRATIVE NOTES.

Note 1, p. 78.—"*Principle of the stereoscope.*"

247. I am sorry to find a notion current among artists, that they can, in some degree, imitate in a picture the effect of the stereoscope, by confusion of lines. There are indeed one or two artifices by which, as stated in the text, an appearance of retirement or projection may be obtained, so that they partly supply the place of the stereoscopic effect, but they do not imitate that effect. The principle of the human sight is simply this :—by means of our two eyes we literally see everything from two places at once; and, by calculated combination, in the brain, of the facts of form so seen, we arrive at conclusions respecting the distance and shape of the object, which we could not otherwise have reached. But it is just as vain to hope

to paint at once the two views of the object as seen
from these two places, though only an inch and a
half distant from each other, as it would be if they
were a mile and a half distant from each other.
With the right eye you see one view of a given
object, relieved against one part of the distance;
with the left eye you see another view of it, relieved against another part of the distance.   You
may paint whichever of those views you please;
you cannot paint both.   Hold your finger upright, between you and this page of the book, about
six inches from your eyes, and three from the
book; shut the right eye, and hide the words
"inches from," in the second line above this, with
your finger; you will then see "six" on one side
of it, and "your," on the other.   Now shut the left
eye and open the right without moving your finger,
and you will see "inches," but not "six."   You
may paint the finger with "inches" beyond it, or
with "six" beyond it, but not with both.   And
this principle holds for any object and any distance.
You might just as well try to paint St. Paul's at once
from both ends of London Bridge as to realise
any stereoscopic effect in a picture.

NOTE 2, p. 106.—"*Dark lines turned to the light.*"

248. It ought to have been farther observed, that
the enclosure of the light by future shadow is by

no means the only reason for the dark lines which great masters often thus introduce. It constantly happens that a local colour will show its own darkness most on the light side, by projecting into and against masses of light in that direction ; and then the painter will indicate this future force of the mass by his dark touch. Both the monk's head in Fig. 11 and dog in Fig. 20 are dark towards the light for this reason.

NOTE 3, p. 177.—" *Softness of reflections.*"

249. I have not quite insisted enough on the extreme care which is necessary in giving the tender evanescence of the edges of the reflections, when the water is in the least agitated ; nor on the decision with which you may reverse the object, when the water is quite calm. Most drawing of reflections is at once confused and hard ; but Nature's is at once intelligible and tender. Generally, at the edge of the water, you ought not to see where reality ceases and reflection begins ; as the image loses itself you ought to keep all its subtle and varied veracities, with the most exquisite softening of its edge. Practise as much as you can from the reflections of ships in calm water, following out all the reversed rigging, and taking, if anything, more pains with the reflection than with the ship.

NOTE 4, p. 180.—" *Where the reflection is darkest,
you will see through the water best.*"

250. For this reason it often happens that if the
water be shallow, and you are looking steeply down
into it, the reflection of objects on the bank will
consist simply of pieces of the bottom seen clearly
through the water, and relieved by flashes of light,
which are the reflection of the sky.   Thus you may
have to draw the reflected dark shape of a bush :
but, inside of that shape, you must not draw the
leaves of the bush, but the stones under the water ;
and, outside of this dark reflection, the blue or
white of the sky, with no stones visible.

NOTE 5, p. 182.—" *Approach streams with
reverence.*"

251. I have hardly said anything about waves of
torrents or waterfalls, as I do not consider them
subjects for beginners to practise upon ; but, as
many of our younger artists are almost breaking
their hearts over them, it may be well to state at
once that it is physically impossible to draw a
running torrent quite rightly, the lustre of its currents and whiteness of its foam being dependent
on intensities of light which art has not at its command.   This also is to be observed, that most
young painters make their defeat certain by attempt-
ing to draw running water, which is a lustrous object

in rapid motion, without ever trying their strength on a lustrous object standing still. Let them break a coarse green-glass bottle into a great many bits, and try to paint those, with all their undulations and edges of fracture, as they lie still on the table ; if they cannot, of course they need not try the rushing crystal and foaming fracture of the stream. If they can manage the glass bottle, let them next buy a fragment or two of yellow fire-opal ; it is quite a common and cheap mineral, and presents, as closely as anything can, the milky bloom and colour of a torrent wave : and if they can conquer the opal, they may at last have some chance with the stream, as far as the stream is in any wise possible. But, as I have just said, the bright parts of it are *not* possible, and ought, as much as may be, to be avoided in choosing subjects. A great deal more may, however, be done than any artist has done yet, in painting the gradual disappearance and lovely colouring of stones seen through clear and calm water.

Students living in towns may make great progress in rock-drawing by frequently and faithfully drawing broken edges of common roofing-slates, of their real size.

Note 6, p. 225.—"*Nature's economy of colour.*"

252. I heard it wisely objected to this statement, the other day, by a young lady, that it was not

through economy that Nature did not colour deep down in the flower bells, but because "she had not light enough there to see to paint with." This may be true; but it is certainly not for want of light that, when she is laying the dark spots on a foxglove, she will not use any more purple than she has got already on the bell, but takes out the colour all round the spot, and concentrates it in the middle.

NOTE 7, p. 249.—" *The law of repetition.*"

253. The reader may perhaps recollect a very beautiful picture of Vandyck's, in the Manchester Exhibition, representing three children in court dresses of rich black and red. The law in question was amusingly illustrated, in the lower corner of that picture, by the introduction of two crows, in a similar colour of court dress, having jet black feathers and bright red beaks.

254. SINCE the first edition of this work was published, I have ascertained that there are two series of engravings from the Bible drawings mentioned in the list at p. 91. One of these is inferior to the other, and in many respects false to the drawings; the "Jericho," for instance, in

the false series, has common bushes instead of
palm trees in the middle distance. The original
plates may be had at almost any respectable
printseller's; and ordinary impressions, whether
of these or any other plates mentioned in the list
at p. 90, will be quite as useful as proofs: but, in
buying Liber Studiorum, it is always well to get
the best impressions that can be had, and if possible impressions of the original plates, published
by Turner. In case these are not to be had,
the copies which are in course of publication by
Mr. Lupton (4 Keppel Street, Russell Square) are
good and serviceable; but no others are of any
use.—[Note of 1857.]

I have placed in the hands of Mr. Ward (Working
Men's College) some photographs from the etchings
made by Turner for the Liber; the original etchings
being now unobtainable, except by fortunate acci-
dent. I have selected the subjects carefully from
my own collection of the etchings; and though
some of the more subtle qualities of line are lost
in the photographs, the student will find these
proofs the best lessons in pen-drawing accessible
to him.—[Note of 1859; see under Mr. Ward's
name in the Index.]

II.

THINGS TO BE STUDIED.

255. The worst danger by far, to which a solitary student is exposed, is that of liking things that he should not. It is not so much his difficulties, as his tastes, which he must set himself to conquer : and although, under the guidance of a master, many works of art may be made instructive, which are only of partial excellence (the good and bad of them being duly distinguished), his safeguard, as long as he studies alone, will be in allowing himself to possess only things, in their way, so free from faults, that nothing he copies in them can seriously mislead him, and to contemplate only those works of art which he knows to be either perfect or noble in their errors.   I will therefore set down, in clear order, the names of the masters whom you may safely admire, and a few of the books which you may safely possess.   In these days of cheap illustration, the danger is always rather of your possessing too much than too little.   It may admit of some question, how far the looking at bad art may set off and illustrate the characters of the good ; but, on the whole, I believe it is best to live always on quite wholesome food, and that our enjoyment of it will never be made more acute by feeding on ashes ; though it may be well sometimes to taste the ashes, in order to know the bitterness of them.

Of course the works of the great masters can only be serviceable to the student after he has made considerable progress himself. It only wastes the time and dulls the feelings of young persons, to drag them through picture galleries; at least, unless they themselves wish to look at particular pictures. Generally, young people only care to enter a picture gallery when there is a chance of getting leave to run a race to the other end of it; and they had better do that in the garden below. If, however, they have any real enjoyment of pictures, and want to look at this one or that, the principal point is never to disturb them in looking at what interests them, and never to make them look at what does not. Nothing is of the least use to young people (nor, by the way, of much use to old ones), but what interests them; and therefore, though it is of great importance to put nothing but good art into their possession, yet, when they are passing through great houses or galleries, they should be allowed to look precisely at what pleases them: if it is not useful to them as art, it will be in some other way; and the healthiest way in which art can interest them is when they look at it, not as art, but because it represents something they like in Nature. If a boy has had his heart filled by the life of some great man, and goes up thirstily to a Vandyck portrait of him, to see what he was like, that is the wholesomest way in which he can begin the study

Y

of portraiture; if he loves mountains, and dwells on a Turner drawing because he sees in it a likeness to a Yorkshire scar or an Alpine pass, that is the wholesomest way in which he can begin the study of landscape; and if a girl's mind is filled with dreams of angels and saints, and she pauses before an Angelico because she thinks it must surely be like heaven, that is the right way for her to begin the study of religious art.

256. When, however, the student has made some definite progress, and every picture becomes really a guide to him, false or true, in his own work, it is of great importance that he should never look, with even partial admiration, at bad art; and then, if the reader is willing to trust me in the matter, the following advice will be useful to him. In which, with his permission, I will quit the indirect and return to the epistolary address, as being the more convenient.

First, in Galleries of Pictures:

1. You may look, with trust in their being always right, at Titian, Veronese, Tintoret, Giorgione, John Bellini, and Velasquez; the authenticity of the picture being of course established for you by proper authority.

2. You may look with admiration, admitting, however, question of right and wrong,[1] at Van Eyck,

[1] I do not mean necessarily to imply inferiority of rank in saying that this second class of painters have questionable

Holbein, Perugino, Francia, Angelico, Leonardo da
Vinci, Correggio, Vandyck, Rembrandt, Reynolds,
Gainsborough, Turner, and the modern Pre-
Raphaelites.[2] You had better look at no other
painters than these, for you run a chance, otherwise, of being led far off the road, or into griev-
ous faults, by some of the other great ones, as
Michael Angelo, Raphael, and Rubens ; and of
being, besides, corrupted in taste by the base ones,
as Murillo, Salvator, Claude, Gaspar Poussin,
Teniers, and such others. You may look, however, for examples of evil, with safe universality of
reprobation, being sure that everything you see is
bad, at Domenichino, the Carracci, Bronzino, and
the figure pieces of Salvator.

Among those named for study under question,
you cannot look too much at, nor grow too
enthusiastically fond of, Angelico, Correggio,
Reynolds, Turner, and the Pre-Raphaelites ; but,
if you find yourself getting especially fond of any
of the others, leave off looking at them, for you
must be going wrong some way or other. If, for
instance, you begin to like Rembrandt or Leonardo

qualities. The greatest men have often many faults, and
sometimes their faults are a part of their greatness ; but such
men are not, of course, to be looked upon by the student
with absolute implicitness of faith.

[2] Including, under this term, John Lewis, and William
Hunt of the Old Water-colour, who, take him all in all, is
the best painter of still life, I believe, that ever existed.

especially, you are losing your feeling for colour; if you like Van Eyck or Perugino especially, you must be getting too fond of rigid detail; and if you like Vandyck or Gainsborough especially, you must be too much attracted by gentlemanly flimsiness.

257. Secondly, of published, or otherwise multiplied, art, such as you may be able to get yourself, or to see at private houses or in shops, the works of the following masters are the most desirable, after the Turners, Rembrandts, and Dürers, which I have asked you to get first :

1. Samuel Prout.[1]

All his published lithographic sketches are of the greatest value, wholly unrivalled in power of composition, and in love and feeling of architectural subject. His somewhat mannered linear execution, though not to be imitated in your own sketches from Nature, may be occasionally copied, for discipline's sake, with great advantage : it will give you a peculiar steadiness of hand, not quickly attainable in any other way; and there is no fear

---

[1] The order in which I place these masters does not in the least imply superiority or inferiority. I wrote their names down as they occurred to me ; putting Rossetti's last because what I had to say of him was connected with other subjects ; and one or another will appear to you great, or be found by you useful, according to the kind of subjects you are studying.

of your getting into any faultful mannerism as long as you carry out the different modes of more delicate study above recommended.

If you are interested in architecture, and wish to make it your chief study, you should draw much from photographs of it; and then from the architecture itself, with the same completion of detail and gradation, only keeping the shadows of due paleness,—in photographs they are always about four times as dark as they ought to be,—and treat buildings with as much care and love as artists do their rock foregrounds, drawing all the moss, and weeds, and stains upon them. But if, without caring to understand architecture, you merely want the picturesque character of it, and to be able to sketch it fast, you cannot do better than take Prout for your exclusive master; only do not think that you are copying Prout by drawing straight lines with dots at the end of them. Get first his " Rhine," and draw the subjects that have most hills, and least architecture in them, with chalk on smooth paper, till you can lay on his broad flat tints, and get his gradations of light, which are very wonderful; then take up the architectural subjects in the " Rhine," and draw again and again the groups of figures, &c., in his "Microcosm," and "Lessons on Light and Shadow." After that, proceed to copy the grand subjects in the " Sketches in Flanders and Germany;" or "in

Switzerland and Italy," if you cannot get the
Flanders; but the Switzerland is very far inferior.
Then work from Nature, not trying to Proutise
Nature, by breaking smooth buildings into rough
ones, but only drawing *what you see*, with Prout's
simple method and firm lines.   Don't copy his
coloured works.   They are good, but not at all equal
to his chalk and pencil drawings; and you will
become a mere imitator, and a very feeble imitator,
if you use colour at all in Prout's method.   I have
not space to explain why this is so, it would take a
long piece of reasoning; trust me for the statement.

2. John Lewis.

His sketches in Spain, lithographed by himself,
are very valuable.   Get them, if you can, and also
some engravings (about eight or ten, I think,
altogether) of wild beasts, executed by his own
hand a long time ago; they are very precious in
every way.   The series of the "Alhambra" is
rather slight, and few of the subjects are lithographed by himself; still it is well worth having.

But let *no* lithographic work come into the
house, if you can help it, nor even look at any,
except Prout's, and those sketches of Lewis's.

3. George Cruikshank.

If you ever happen to meet with the two volumes of "Grimm's German Stories," which were
illustrated by him long ago, pounce upon them

instantly ; the etchings in them are the finest things, next to Rembrandt's, that, as far as I know, have been done since etching was invented. You cannot look at them too much, nor copy them too often.

All his works are very valuable, though disagreeable when they touch on the worst vulgarities of modern life; and often much spoiled by a curiously mistaken type of face, divided so as to give too much to the mouth and eyes and leave too little for forehead, the eyes being set about two thirds up, instead of at half the height of the head. But his manner of work is always right ; and his tragic power, though rarely developed, and warped by habits of caricature, is, in reality, as great as his grotesque power.

There is no fear of his hurting your taste, as long as your principal work lies among art of so totally different a character as most of that which I have recommended to you ; and you may, therefore, get great good by copying almost anything of his that may come in your way; except only his illustrations, lately published, to " Cinderella," and " Jack and the Bean-stalk," and " Tom Thumb," which are much over-laboured, and confused in line. You should get them, but do not copy them.

4. Alfred Rethel.

I only know two publications by him ; one, the " Dance of Death," with text by Reinick, published

in Leipsic, but to be had now of any London
bookseller for the sum, I believe, of eighteen
pence, and containing six plates full of instructive
character; the other, of two plates only, "Death
the Avenger," and "Death the Friend." These
two are far superior to the "Todtentanz," and, if
you can get them, will be enough in themselves to
show all that Rethel can teach you. If you dislike
ghastly subjects, get "Death the Friend" only.

5. Bewick.

The execution of the plumage in Bewick's birds
is the most masterly thing ever yet done in wood-
cutting; it is worked just as Paul Veronese would
have worked in wood, had he taken to it. His
vignettes, though too coarse in execution, and
vulgar in types of form, to be good copies, show,
nevertheless, intellectual power of the highest
order; and there are pieces of sentiment in them,
either pathetic or satirical, which have never since
been equalled in illustrations of this simple kind;
the bitter intensity of the feeling being just like
that which characterises some of the leading Pre-
Raphaelites. Bewick is the Burns of painting.

6. Blake.

The "Book of Job," engraved by himself, is of
the highest rank in certain characters of imagination and expression; in the mode of obtaining
certain effects of light it will also be a very useful

example to you. In expressing conditions of glaring and flickering light, Blake is greater than Rembrandt.

7. Richter.

I have already told you what to guard against in looking at his works. I am a little doubtful whether I have done well in including them in this catalogue at all; but the imaginations in them are so lovely and numberless, that I must risk, for their sake, the chance of hurting you a little in judgment of style. If you want to make presents of story-books to children, his are the best you can now get; but his most beautiful work, as far as I know, is his series of Illustrations to the Lord's Prayer.

8. Rossetti.

An edition of Tennyson, lately published, contains woodcuts from drawings by Rossetti and other chief Pre Raphaelite masters. They are terribly spoiled in the cutting, and generally the best part, the expression of feature, *entirely* lost;[2] still they are full of instruction, and cannot be studied too

---

[2] This is especially the case in the St. Cecily, Rossetti's first illustration to the "Palace of Art," which would have been the best in the book had it been well engraved. The whole work should be taken up again, and done by line engraving, perfectly; and wholly from Pre-Raphaelite designs, with which no other modern work can bear the least comparison.

closely. But observe, respecting these woodcuts, that if you have been in the habit of looking at much spurious work, in which sentiment, action, and style are borrowed or artificial, you will assuredly be offended at first by all genuine work, which is intense in feeling. Genuine art, which is merely art, such as Veronese's or Titian's, may not offend you, though the chances are that you will not care about it; but genuine works of feeling, such as "Maud" or "Aurora Leigh" in poetry, or the grand Pre-Raphaelite designs in painting, are sure to offend you: and if you cease to work hard, and persist in looking at vicious and false art, they will continue to offend you. It will be well, therefore, to have one type of entirely false art, in order to know what to guard against. Flaxman's outlines to Dante contain, I think, examples of almost every kind of falsehood and feebleness which it is possible for a trained artist, not base in thought, to commit or admit, both in design and execution. Base or degraded choice of subject, such as you will constantly find in Teniers and others of the Dutch painters, I need not, I hope, warn you against; you will simply turn away from it in disgust; while mere bad or feeble drawing, which makes mistakes in every direction at once, cannot teach you the particular sort of educated fallacy in question. But, in these designs of Flaxman's, you have gentlemanly feeling, and fair knowledge of anatomy, and firm setting down of lines, all applied in the foolishest and worst possible way; you cannot have a more finished example of learned error, amiable want of meaning, and bad drawing with a steady hand.[3] Retzsch's outlines have more real material in them

[3] The praise I have given incidentally to Flaxman's sculpture in the "Seven Lamps," and elsewhere, refers wholly to his studies from Nature, and simple groups in marble, which were always good and interesting. Still, I have overrated him, even in this respect; and it is generally to be remembered that, in speaking of artists whose works I cannot be supposed to have specially studied, the errors I fall into will always be on the side of praise. For, of course, praise is most likely to be given when the thing praised is above one's knowledge; and, therefore, as our knowledge increases, such things may be found less praiseworthy than we thought. But blame can only be justly given when the thing blamed is below one's level of sight; and, practically, I never do blame anything until I have got well past it, and am certain that there is demonstrable falsehood in it. I believe, therefore, all my blame to be wholly trustworthy, having never yet had occasion to repent of one depreciatory word that I have ever written, while I have often found that, with respect to things I had not time to study closely, I was led too far by sudden admiration, helped, perhaps, by peculiar associations, or other deceptive accidents; and this the more, because I never care to check an expression of delight, thinking the chances are, that, even if mistaken, it will do more good than harm; but I weigh every word of blame with scrupulous caution. I have sometimes erased a strong passage of blame from second editions of my books; but this was only when I found it offended the reader without convincing him, never because I repented of it myself.

than Flaxman's, occasionally showing true fancy and power; in artistic principle they are nearly as bad, and in taste, worse. All outlines from statuary, as given in works on classical art, will be very hurtful to you if you in the least like them; and *nearly* all finished line engravings. Some particular prints I could name which possess instructive qualities, but it would take too long to distinguish them, and the best way is to avoid line engravings of figures altogether.[4] If you happen to be a rich person, possessing quantities of them, and if you are fond of the large finished prints from Raphael, Correggio, &c., it is wholly impossible that you can make any progress in knowledge of real art till you have sold them all,—or burnt them, which would be a greater benefit to the world. I hope that, some day, true and noble engravings will be made from the few pictures of the great schools, which the restorations undertaken by the modern managers of foreign galleries may leave us; but the existing engravings have nothing whatever in common with the good in the works they profess to represent, and, if you like them, you like in the originals of them hardly anything but their errors.

[4] Large line engravings, I mean, in which the lines, as such, are conspicuous. Small vignettes in line are often beautiful in figures no less than landscape; as, for instance, those from Stothard's drawings in Rogers's Italy; and, therefore, I have just recommended the vignettes to Tennyson to be done by line engraving.

258. Finally, your judgment will be, of course, much affected by your taste in literature. Indeed, I know many persons who have the purest taste in literature, and yet false taste in art, and it is a phenomenon which puzzles me not a little; but I have never known any one with false taste in books, and true taste in pictures. It is also of the greatest importance to you, not only for art's sake, but for all kinds of sake, in these days of book deluge, to keep out of the salt swamps of literature, and live on a little rocky island of your own, with a spring and a lake in it, pure and good. I cannot, of course, suggest the choice of your library to you: every several mind needs different books; but there are some books which we all need, and assuredly, if you read Homer,[1] Plato, Æschylus, Herodotus, Dante,[2] Shakspeare, and Spenser, as much as you ought, you will not require wide enlargement of shelves to right and left of them for purposes of perpetual study. Among modern books avoid generally magazine and review literature. Sometimes it may contain a useful

[1] Chapman's, if not the original.
[2] Cary's or Cayley's, if not the original. I do not know which are the best translations of Plato. Herodutus and Æschylus can only be read in the original. It may seem strange that I name books like these for "beginners:" but all the greatest books contain food for all ages; and an intelligent and rightly bred youth or girl ought to enjoy much, even in Plato, by the time they are fifteen or sixteen.

abridgment or a wholesome piece of criticism;
but the chances are ten to one it will either waste
your time or mislead you.   If you want to understand any subject whatever, read the best book
upon it you can hear of : not a review of the book.
If you don't like the first book you try, seek for
another ; but do not hope ever to understand the
subject without pains, by a reviewer's help.   Avoid
especially that class of literature which has a
knowing tone ; it is the most poisonous of all.
Every good book, or piece of book, is full of admiration and awe ; it may contain firm assertion or
stern satire, but it never sneers coldly, nor asserts
haughtily, and it always leads you to reverence or
love something with your whole heart.   It is not
always easy to distinguish the satire of the venomous
race of books from the satire of the noble and pure
ones ; but in general you may notice that the cold-
blooded, Crustacean and Batrachian books will
sneer at sentiment ; and the warm-blooded, human
books, at sin.   Then, in general, the more you can
restrain your serious reading to reflective or lyric
poetry, history, and natural history, avoiding fiction
and the drama, the healthier your mind will become.
Of modern poetry, keep to Scott, Wordsworth,
Keats, Crabbe, Tennyson, the two Brownings,
Thomas Hood, Lowell, Longfellow, and Coventry
Patmore, whose "Angel in the House" is a most
finished piece of writing, and the sweetest analysis

we possess of quiet modern domestic feeling ; while
Mrs. Browning's " Aurora Leigh " is, as far as I
know, the greatest poem which the century has produced in any language. Cast Coleridge at once
aside, as sickly and useless ; and Shelley, as shallow
and verbose ; Byron, until your taste is fully formed,
and you are able to discern the magnificence in him
from the wrong. Never read bad or common poetry,
nor write any poetry yourself ; there is, perhaps,
rather too much than too little in the world already.

259. Of reflective prose, read chiefly Bacon,
Johnson, and Helps. Carlyle is hardly to be
named as a writer for " beginners," because his
teaching, though to some of us vitally necessary,
may to others be hurtful. If you understand and
like him, read him ; if he offends you, you are not
yet ready for him, and perhaps may never be so ;
at all events, give him up, as you would sea-bathing
if you found it hurt you, till you are stronger. Of
fiction, read "Sir Charles Grandison," Scott's
novels, Miss Edgeworth's, and, if you are a young
lady, Madame de Genlis', the French Miss Edgeworth ; making these, I mean, your constant companions. Of course you must, or will, read other
books for amusement once or twice ; but you will
find that these have an element of perpetuity in
them, existing in nothing else of their kind ; while
their peculiar quietness and repose of manner will
also be of the greatest value in teaching you to feel

the same characters in art.   Read little at a time, trying to feel interest in little things, and reading not so much for the sake of the story as to get acquainted with the pleasant people into whose company these writers bring you.   A common book will often give you much amusement, but it is only a noble book which will give you dear friends.   Remember, also, that it is of less import- ance to you in your earlier years, that the books you read should be clever than that they should be right.   I do not mean oppressively or repulsively instructive; but that the thoughts they express should be just, and the feelings they excite generous. It is not necessary for you to read the wittiest or the most suggestive books : it is better, in general, to hear what is already known, and may be simply said.   Much of the literature of the present day, though good to be read by persons of ripe age, has a tendency to agitate rather than confirm, and leaves its readers too frequently in a helpless or hopeless indignation, the worst possible state into which the mind of youth can be thrown.   It may, indeed, become necessary for you, as you advance in life, to set your hand to things that need to be altered in the world, or apply your heart chiefly to what must be pitied in it, or condemned ; but, for a young person, the safest temper is one of reverence, and the safest place one of obscurity. Certainly at present, and perhaps through all your life, your teachers are wisest when they make you content in quiet virtue, and that literature and art are best for you which point out, in common life, and in familiar things, the objects for hopeful labour, and for humble love.

COLLATION OF THE EDITIONS.

———▸◂———

[The Bibliographical Note at the beginning of
this volume will perhaps suffice for the general
reader: fuller information is given in Mr. T. J.
Wise's "Bibliography of Ruskin," Part III.   In
the following notes, mere typographical differences
—in italics, punctuation, and pagination—are not
noticed.]

Preface, p. xviii. (§ ix.) ; edd. 1 and 2 omit footnote.

P. 48 (§ 47), line 16 ; ed. 1 reads "Now, I do not
want you to copy Fig. 5, but to copy the stone
before you in the way that Fig. 5 is done." And,
line 23, "scrawling the paper all over, round it,
as at *b*, Fig. 5.   You cannot rightly see what the
form of the stone really is till you begin finishing,
so sketch it in quite rudely ; only rather leave
too *much* room," &c.

P. 49 (§ 47), line 6 ; ed. 1 reads "it is impossible for
you to draw that shape quite truly."

P. 50 (§ 47), line 1 ; ed. 1 reads "For instance, I was
going to draw, beside *a*, another effect on the
stone, reflected light," &c.

P. 60 (§ 59), line 13 ; ed. 1 omits "*a* in" before
"Fig. 1."

P. 65 (§ 63), line 21 ; edd. 1 and 2 read "pre-liminarily."

P. 66 (§ 64), line 1 ; ed. 1 reads " Prepare your colour as before directed."

P. 71 (§ 69), line 13 ; ed. 1 reads " Nothing but practice will do this perfectly ; but you will often save," &c.

P. 75 (§ 71 *n*), line 15 ; edd. 1, 2, 3 read "the most neglected is," in this ed. altered to "the most neglected was."

P. 78 (§ 75 *n*), last line ; ed. 1 omits "see, however, Note 1, in Appendix I."

P. 85 (§ 81), line 2 ; ed. 1 reads "take one of the *drawings*, and put it," &c.

P. 90 (§ 86), line 4 ; ed. 1 reads " each letter—of course the plates marked with two or three letters are, for the most part, the best. Do not get more," &c.

P. 90 (§ 86), line 7 ; for " The plates marked . . . . Appendix I," ed. 1 reads " If you can, get first the plates marked with a star," and omits the star after " Dartmouth Cove" and " Launceston."

P. 91 (§ 86 *n*), line 10 ; ed. 1 omits star after " Drachenfels."

P. 91 (§ 86 *n*), line 18 ; ed. 1 omits star after " Melrose."

P. 91 (§ 86 *n*), line 19 ; ed. 2 omits star after " Dry-burgh."

P. 91 (§ 86 *n*), line 19 ; ed. 1 omits star after " Loch Coriskin."

P. 106 (§ 97 *n*), last line ; ed. 1 omits note.

P. 112 (§ 99), last line but three ; edd. 1, 2, 3 read "*News* or *Times*," in this ed. altered to " *News* or others."

P. 127 (§ 107), line 22 ; ed. 1 reads " The figure 20."

P. 137 (§ 111), line 15 ; edd. 1, 2, 3 read " St. Catherine, lately photographed." In this ed. "lately" is omitted.

P. 177 (§ 142), last line ; ed. 1 omits footnote.

P. 180 (§ 145), last line ; ed. 1 omits footnote.

P. 182 (§ 146) ; ed. 1 omits footnote 1.

P. 225 (§ 175), last line ; ed. 1 omits footnote.

P. 249 (§ 197), last line ; ed. 1 omits footnote.

P. 266 (§ 207), line 5 ; ed. 3 reads "forest of mountain," a misprint for "forest or mountain."

P. 315 (§ 241), lines 10 to 16 ; ed. 1 reads "Among those which I never hope to explain, are chiefly laws of expression, and others bearing simply on simple matters ; but, for that very reason, more influential than any others. These are, from the first, as inexplicable as our bodily sensations are, it being just as impossible, I think, to explain why one succession," &c.

Pp. 329-335, Appendix I. (§§ 247-254), omitted in ed. 1.

P. 335, lines 15-24 (second paragraph in § 254), omitted in ed. 2.

P. 336 (§ 255), last line but three ; ed. 1 reads "by feeding, however temporarily, on ashes. Of course the works," &c.

P. 340 (§ 257) ; ed. 1 omits footnote.

P. 345 (§ 257), line 8 ; ed. 1 reads "but the fancies in them are so pretty and numberless," and omits at end of paragraph "but his most beautiful work . . . Lord's Prayer."

P. 348 (§ 257 n^4) ; ed. 1 omits footnote 4.

P. 350 (§ 258), line 4 from bottom ; edd. 1 and 2 omit "Thomas Hood."

INDEX.

---

* "Thus far I have repeated, with modification of two sentences only,
the words of my old 'Elements of Drawing;'—words which I could
not change to any good purpose, so far as they are addressed to the
modern amateur. . . . But the Laws of Fésole address themselves to no
persons of such temper ; they are written only for students who have
the fortitude to do their best ; and I am not minded any more, as will
be seen in next chapter, while they have any store of round sixpences in
their pockets, to allow them to draw their sun, earth, or moon like
crooked ones."—*Laws of Fésole*, viii. 5.

Rubens, Spagnoletto, Stothard, Teniers, Tintoret, Titian, Turner, Van Eyck, Vandyck, Velasquez, Wilson.

Arundel, Turner's, 86 *n.*

Arveron, Turner's Source of the, 109 *n*[2], 151.

Ashby de la Zouche, Turner's, 86 *n.*

Association does not create beauty, 120.

Attention disciplined by study with the point, 6.

Augsburg, Prout's, 220.

Aurora Leigh, Mrs. Browning's, 257 *seq.*

Author : *personal:* taught by Mr. Runciman, xiii. *n* ; teaches at the Working Men's College, ix. His study of the methods of colouring, 158 ; would tax colours, 171 *n.* He errs rather by praising than by blaming too much, 257 *n*[3]. Appoints Mr. W. Ward his substitute for answering letters, xv.; and providing copies from Liber Studiorum, 254.

Works. "Modern Painters," vol. I. ii. 6 (pp. 382–400), praises Harding's foliage, 128.

"Modern Painters," vol. IV. plate 21 (p. 22), illustrating ground, 147.

"Modern Painters," vol. IV. chap. 3, on tone, 236 *n.*

"Modern Painters," vol. IV. chap. 4, on mystery, 138 *n.*

"Modern Painters," vol. IV. chap. 8, § 6, on composition, 189.

"Modern Painters," vol. IV. chap. 17, on curves, 207 *n.*

"Stones of Venice," vol. III. chap. 1, § 8, on curves, 207 *n.*

"Seven Lamps of Architecture," chap. i. § x., praises Flaxman,* 257 *n*[3].

"Harbours of England," Scarborough, on repose, 197.

"Elements of Drawing:" additions to ed. 2 ; advt. to 2nd ed. (and see the Collation prefixed to this Index).

For whose use written, ii. viii. *seqq.*, 3 (and see note to *Accuracy* in this Index) ; does not teach the Author's final method of teaching, iv.; nor exactly reproduce his method at the Working Men's College, ix. *seq.* It aims at teaching observation of Nature, viii.; promises no royal road, viii.,

---

* But only in general terms. The passage is :—

"We have so much, suppose, to be spent in decoration ; let us go to the Flaxman of his time, whoever he may be. . . . It may be that we do not desire ornament of so high an order . . . choose, therefore, the Roman hatchet work, instead of the Flaxman frieze and statue."

but the simplest possible, x., xv., and teaches self-help, 1.
Some objections answered, ix. ; apology for slightness of
illustrations, 211 *n.*

5 *n* ; in shades, 55 ; in water, 145 *seq.* " Retiring " colours
and aerial perspective, 184.   Nature's economy, 175, 252 ;
and unpaintable brilliance, 5 *n*, 234 *seqq.*

Study. Children should be allowed "paints," ii. ; the
serious beginner should not, iii. ; tax should be laid on bright
colours, 171 *n.*   Difficulties of colouring ; relativity,* 152.
Local colour sometimes expresses form, 59, and sometimes
conceals it, 183 ; should be rendered in monochrome drawing by tone, 22, 40 ; and studied by scales, 37 *seqq.*, 237.
But colour in shade is not merely a darker tint of the same
hue in light,† 55 ; nor the hue deepened with black, 236 ;
but complicated by reflection, 53 *seqq.*   Power of colouring
necessary to perfect draughtsmanship, 183 *n.*

Method of painting in water-colour.   Importance of neat-
ness and system, iii., 156 ; colour in cakes recommended,‡
24, 121, 156, 163 ; which to use for colour scales, 37 ; and
for general practice, 157, 163.   First practice, 6, 23.   How
to mix colours, 24, 29, 31, 157, 162 *seqq.*, 170.   Use of
body-colour, 157 *seqq.*   Mosaic method, 166.   Various
artifices, 170 *seqq.*   (And see *Water-colour.*)

Sketching from Nature in colour, 153 *seqq.* ; in such
memoranda, form to be neglected, 154 (but see note to
Accuracy in this Index).   Practice of matching colours,
164 ; its importance, 165 ; and insufficiency, owing to the

* The statement in the text is somewhat modified in a note to " Laws
of Fésole," viii. 1 (p. 116).   " Colour is (wholly) relative.—No, not
' wholly ' by any means. . . . Colour is no less positive than line, considered as a representation of fact ; and you either match a given colour,
or do not, as you either draw a given ellipse or square, or do not.   Nor,
on the other hand, are lines, in their grouping, destitute of relative
influence ; they exalt or depress their individual powers by association ;
and the necessity for the correction of the above passage in this respect
was pointed out to me by Miss Hill, many and many a year ago, when
she was using the Elements in teaching design for glass.   But the influence of lines on each other is restricted within narrow limits, while the
sequences of colour are like those of sound, and susceptible of all the
complexity and passion of the most accomplished music."
† Ultimately the Author found it advisable to direct beginners in his
Oxford drawing school to "shade simply with a deeper and (if you
already know what the word means) a warmer tone of the colour you
are using " (*Laws of Fésole*, viii. 9), this being an approach to the
practice of the Venetians, as opposed to that of the Bolognese and
Roman schools (*Lectures on Art*, v. 134).
‡ This was in 1857.   Now that moist water-colours are sold in tubes,
so that they can be set on the palette clean every morning, the tubes are
recommended (*Laws of Fésole*, x. 13).

---

* "A fine work of art differs from a vulgar one by subtleties of line, which the most perfect measurement is not alone delicate enough to detect; but to which precision of attempted measurement directs the attention; while the security of boundaries, within which maximum error *must* be restrained, enables the hand gradually to approach the perfectness which instruments cannot " (*Laws of Fésole*, Preface).

* It must be remembered that this was written in 1857.

Principles and practice of art, Harding's, 137 *n.*
Prints to copy, iii., and see *Engravings.*
Prodigal Son, Rembrandt's etching, 90.
Prout, Samuel, 147 ; draughtsmanship, 18 *n* ; weak in linear perspective, xiii. ; great in composition, 220, 229.
    His writings on composition, 197. Which of his works to study, 257.
Prudhoe Castle, Turner's, 86 *n.*
Prussian blue for first practice,* 24.
Punch newspaper, Leech's drawings, 91.
Puseyism, 244 *n.*

QUILL pen, 108 *seq.*, 150.
Quotations and allusions in this work. To the Author's own works, see *Author.*
    Bottom the weaver (Shakspeare's *Midsummer Night's Dream*), 240.
    Casella, Dante's friend (*Purgatorio*, ii. 91), 240.
    Harding on tree-drawing (*Lessons on Trees*), 129.
    Launce and his dog (Shakspeare's *Two Gentlemen of Verona*, act ii., scene 5), 167.
    Mulready on method (conversation with the author), 160.
    Pope's Essay on Criticism (part i. lines 175-180), 222 *n.*
    Turner, a phrase of his (in conversation), 18.
    Various authors and works recommended, 258 *seq.*

RADIATION, 105, 127 *seqq.*, 210 *seqq.*, 215, 225 ; overruled by caprice and mystery, 130 *seqq.*
Rag, see *Paint-rag.*
Raglan, Turner's, 109 *n* 2.
Raphael, vi., 18 *n*, 93 and fig. 11, 97, 111, 195, 256 *seq.*
Rapidity of execution, 8, 12 and *n*, 116 ; required for sketching clouds, 149.
    Of conception, 137.
Reading for young students, 258 *seq.*
Reasons of natural appearances not required in art, 50.
Refinement important, 45, 58, 60, 69. (See *Delicacy.*)
Reflected light, 53 *seqq.* ; colour, 53 *seqq.*, 238.
Reflections in water, 141 *seqq.*, 249 *seq.*

* The " shilling cake " recommended in the text refers to the form in which the colour was sold in 1857. See under *Colour* in this Index.

* Now of Richmond, and Bedford Chambers, 28 Southampton Street, Strand, London, W.C., still supplies prints and photographs after Turner, &c., to illustrate the Author's works and teaching.

THE END.